THE
HIDDEN POWER
OF THE BIBLE

What *Science of Mind* Reveals
About the Bible and You

JEREMY P. TARCHER/PENGUIN

a member of Penguin Group (USA) Inc.

New York

THE
HIDDEN POWER
OF THE BIBLE

What *Science of Mind* Reveals
About the Bible and You

ORIGINALLY PUBLISHED AS
The Bible in the Light of Religious Science

ERNEST HOLMES

JEREMY P. TARCHER/PENGUIN

Published by the Penguin Group

Penguin Group (USA) Inc., 375 Hudson Street, New York, New York 10014, USA • Penguin Group
(Canada), 90 Eglinton Ave East, Suite 700, Toronto, Ontario M4P 2Y3, Canada (a division of Pearson
Penguin Canada Inc.) • Penguin Books Ltd, 80 Strand, London WC2R 0RL, England • Penguin Ireland,
25 St Stephen's Green, Dublin 2, Ireland (a division of Penguin Books Ltd) • Penguin Group (Australia),
250 Camberwell Road, Camberwell, Victoria 3124, Australia (a division of Pearson Australia Group Pty
Ltd) • Penguin Books India Pvt Ltd, 11 Community Centre, Panchsheel Park, New Delhi–110 017,
India • Penguin Group (NZ), Cnr Airborne and Rosedale Roads, Albany, Auckland 1310,
New Zealand (a division of Pearson New Zealand Ltd) • Penguin Books (South Africa) (Pty) Ltd,
24 Sturdee Avenue, Rosebank, Johannesburg 2196, South Africa

Penguin Books Ltd, Registered Offices:
80 Strand, London WC2R 0RL, England

First edition published in February 1929 as *The Bible in the Light of Religious Science*
This edition © 2006 Jeremy P. Tarcher/Penguin

Most Tarcher/Penguin books are available at special quantity discounts for bulk purchase
for sales promotions, premiums, fund-raising, and educational needs. Special books or book
excerpts also can be created to fit specific needs. For details, write Penguin Group (USA) Inc.
Special Markets, 375 Hudson Street, New York, NY 10014.

Library of Congress Cataloging-in-Publication Data

Holmes, Ernest, 1887–1960
[Bible in the light of religious science]
The hidden power of the Bible : what science of mind reveals about the Bible and you :
originally published as The Bible in the light of religious science / Ernest Holmes.
p.   cm.
Originally published: New York : R.M. McBride, 1929. With new index.
Includes index.
ISBN 1-58542-511-7
1. New Thought.   2. Bible—Criticism, interpretation, etc.   I. Title.
BF639.H615   2006   2006044498
299'.93—dc22

Printed in the United States of America
3   5   7   9   10   8   6   4   2

Book design by Stephanie Huntwork

Preface to the Tarcher / Penguin Edition

Every religion has its exoteric and esoteric—outer and inner—aspects. In religious practice, the exoteric is the body of rote and ritual, done singly or with others, whereas the esoteric is everything that happens within the participants. The relationship between the two is the same as that between a map and a journey, or between a lecture on happiness and being genuinely happy. Singing a hymn is an exoteric activity. Loving or hating that hymn, or dissolving into tears at the dawning awareness of the presence of Deity, is a possible hymn-driven esoteric response.

Utterly unpredictable, the esoteric event of being swept up in a wave of spiritual feeling and intimate self-awareness may accompany or follow some act of spiritual discipline, or may suddenly appear from nowhere, the way characters "apparate" every now and then around Harry Potter. People whose spiritual lives are punctuated by esoteric moments cannot just turn off what they have felt and known, nor can they satisfactorily explain it to themselves, much less to anyone else. Thus, religion's esoteric core has built a reputation for secrecy. This is a clever diversionary tactic: It isn't so much that such things should not be talked about among the rote-bound profane. It's that they *cannot* be. There are literally no words to describe them, for they are glimpses of the Infinite, around which no circle can be drawn.

Although esotericism is typically handled like a controlled substance by Western religion, every enduring formal religious practice was cast in place because at some time, somebody received a new and life-altering insight into the heart of timeless reality while reciting those words, or consecrating that Host, or sitting in that asana. Centuries along, the antecedent may have been lost, as practices became engaged for tradition's sake and nothing more. Still, at this very moment, somebody saying a familiar prayer abruptly becomes that prayer, and its answer—all of this occurring so immediately and so completely that the new state of consciousness feels like the only one ever inhabited. This is the truth of esoteric experience.

When asked by the king to get on with it in summarizing his mathematical theory, Euclid replied, "There is no royal road to geometry." Nothing happens without the investment of the self. Grasp the point and it can then extend to a line, then a plane, then a solid. Put another way, only the mind moves. Maps and lectures suggest actions they themselves cannot take, as do our world's volumes of sacred law. There is no road to the attainment of goals, or peace of mind, or anything else, that does not lead through the self. We often wish somebody else could take us where we want to go; discovering they cannot, we dismiss them and hunt for another.

This book's author, Ernest Holmes, detected a deeper current in life—and ultimately founded a new religion based on it. He did so after insisting for years that the world had an ample supply of wisdom traditions, ready and waiting to be used, and pointed out that same truths could be found in any of them, if one would only look.

The Judeo-Christian Bible has never lifted a spirit: Those countless spirits have lifted *themselves,* by contemplating biblical meanings and their application, prying themselves out of submergence in evident mortality and meaninglessness, lifting up inner eyes "unto the hills" as an achievement of belief, the result of thought uniting with emotion. The Bible itself is a sometime historical record, woven together with myth, legend, hyperbole, civic ordinances, genealogy, military strategy, a lot of political maneuvering, some romance, much brutality and—probably most of all—hope for a better world, with emphatic ideas on how to go about building one. For practical reasons if none other, it is the most significant work ever compiled, the most exquisite illustration ever rendered of a world long past that nevertheless mirrors our own, and that from the standpoint of collective consciousness subtly influences everyone's thinking, even those who would deny its existence.

In this interpretation of the Bible by Ernest Holmes, there are certain things you will not find, which you should probably note if you are familiar with biblical exegesis. Holmes's contents here are of the interior type—that is, they lead in rather than out. Holmes did not read Greek, Hebrew, or Aramaic. He possessed no seminary credentials, or much in the way of any formal education. He was deeply interested in the Bible, but also in the Vedas, the Gathas and Avestas, and the Gnostic trove found during his lifetime at Nag Hammadi. What's more, he was a voracious student of life and particularly of what people thought and felt and cared about, and he saw a commonality in human hopes and dreams that determined him to spend his life exploring how best those dreams might be realized. This led him to piece together a philosophy he called the Science of Mind—"a correlation of the laws of science, opinions of philosophy, and revelations of religion, applied to the needs and aspirations of humankind." This philosophy has quietly helped shape the body of work we know as the human potential movement.

Holmes's "leading-into" approach to Scripture subjectively involves—no, engulfs—the reader. At every turn it invites us to wonder what a passage might mean to us personally, rather than being told what it must mean to everybody. Holmes's contemporary Charles Fillmore, a teacher and philosopher who cofounded the Unity movement, did the same, taking the names of the twelve Disciples and extracting a particular spiritual quality and moral lesson from each, which he offered up as food for thought. Emma Curtis Hopkins, of whom both Fillmore and Holmes were briefly students, also did this with the twelve precious gems that adorn the foundation of Jerusalem's walls in the Book of Revelation. All three teachers speculated about meanings to be found in the number twelve. None of this is to say Holmes lacked a decisive position. His was simply this: God is all there is. Therefore, we are each made up of God. Our suffering derives from a sense of separation from our Source, which boils down to misdirected belief. Holmes taught that prayer "in faith, believing"—i.e., believing that something will absolutely happen—is the means to restore our sense of oneness with our Creator and thereby with all creation.

You won't be far into this book when you realize that the hidden power of the Bible is not ultimately about the Bible, nor is it hidden, but rather exists in plain view for those who endeavor to see. It is definitely power, though: your power and my power to enhance the quality of our own lives, and each other's lives, and our planetary life, by coming home to ourselves, using the Bible's record of unfolding awareness as a working tool in the rebuilding and beautification of our own inner temple. May you greatly enjoy and richly benefit from the undertaking.

Jesse Jennings, D.D.
Spring, Texas

Contents

From the Teachings of Moses
the Great Lawgiver

READINGS FROM THE NEW TESTAMENT

From the Teachings of Jesus

From the Epistles of the Apostles

Foreword

Religious Science is the science of mind and Spirit, a culmination of the age-long search for Truth. Those responsible for this movement lay no claim to any special dispensation of Providence, nor a special revelation of Truth. Religious Science contains the best thought of the ages and presents this thought in a manner that can be understood by all.

Religious Science is psychological, metaphysical, mental, spiritual, idealistic, and practical. It is psychological as it deals with the operations of the human mind, metaphysical as it shows the human mind to be an extension of the Divine Mind. The human mind is an instrument through which the Divine Mind functions on the plane of individual life.

Religious Science is mental since it deals with the law of mind, the most subtle energy known. It is spiritual because it reveals a Universal Spirit inherent in all things. It is idealistic, teaching the greatest ideals ever perceived, and practical because it provides a way by which one may attain these ideals.

Religious Science is a science of correct thinking and living. Being a science of correct thinking it is a science of health, happiness, and success; of peace, poise and power, satisfaction and attainment. It is the Science of Being.

Every man is in search of Truth, of something that will make him happy, certain of himself and of life. The very fact that everyone is seeking Truth proves that it exists for all. The universe plays no favorites, has no pets. The Truth is free to all and "whosoever will, may come."

We see an abundance in the universe. The ocean is filled with fish. We cannot count the grains of sand on the shore. The earth contains untold riches and the very air is vibrant with power. Why, then, is man weak, poor, and afraid? Religious Science answers these questions.

The Divine Plan is one of freedom; bondage was not God-ordained. Freedom is the birthright of every living soul. All instinctively feel this. The Truth points a way to freedom under law.

What is Religion? The dictionary tells us that religion is a man's belief in God or gods. Everyone believes in some kind of a god, therefore, everyone has some kind of religion. In so far as anyone's belief in God is correct his religion is true and pure, no matter what outward form it takes.

We need not be afraid of religion. What we wish to avoid is not religion, but dogmatism and superstition. We avoid these by keeping faith with reason, for she converts the soul to reality, gives peace to the understanding, and joy to the heart.

We all wish to be scientific for science is exact knowledge, and knowledge gives power. We live in a scientific age, therefore in an age of greater recognition of truth. Whatever is true in any religion constitutes the science of that religion. We need a science of religion and a religion of science.

Psychology is the study of the human mind. We all desire to understand how the mind works. Everyone should be, to some degree, a psychologist. It is one of the most interesting, fascinating, and practical studies known.

Metaphysics is the study of the relationship between the human and the Divine Mind. It is an extension of psychology and a logical one. We could not have human minds unless there were a First Mind behind ours.

What does it mean to be spiritual? Spirituality is common goodness, human kindness, natural truth, brotherly love, and heavenly worship. To be spiritual is to be normal. All people are spiritual part of the time; some people are spiritual nearly all of the time.

An idealist need not be an empty-minded dreamer but one who sees a greater possibility in the things he does. Our best artists, poets, writers, statesmen, philosophers, and business men are all idealists along their own lines.

Strange as it may appear, the Bible contains a key to health, happiness, and success. It promises more than any other book ever written. It tells how to obtain and what to avoid. When understood, the Bible is a scientific text book.

But the Bible presents its truths in a mystical manner; its meaning is hidden behind story and fable, word pictures, and figures of speech. We must seek its hidden meaning and reveal the purpose underlying its teaching.

The Bible is a book pointing a way to freedom under law, to guidance under love, to revelation through reason. Let us approach its study with this in mind and much will become clear which otherwise seems confusing.

The two great teachers of the Bible are Moses and Jesus. Moses taught the universal law of cause and effect. Jesus tells us of a direct relationship between God and man. One is not complete without the other. Both teachings are necessary. We are individuals living in a universe of law and order; a perfectly balanced, normal viewpoint, connecting life with living, is, in the last analysis, what we are all seeking.

In compiling the following pages an endeavor has been made to avoid details, repetition, and dogma, and to incorporate passages from "The Grand Old Book," which time cannot change nor environment alter; for, built upon the rock of changeless and eternal Reality, self-evident truths cannot be shaken.

The Bible is a compilation of writings extending over a period of many hundreds of years. The following excerpts have made a strong appeal to me because of their uplifting character and I feel that students of Religious Science will find them to be a constant source of spiritual strength and enlightenment.

The Bible was written by human beings whose thought was reaching toward Ultimate Reality, and, if it is to be understood, it must be read with the same motive. Always, the mind that writes is the mind that reads, for there is but One Mind in the universe and all inquiry into Truth is an inquiry into this Mind.

ERNEST S. HOLMES

Los Angeles, California

1928

READINGS FROM THE OLD TESTAMENT

FROM THE STORY OF CREATION

In the beginning God created the heaven and the earth.

And the earth was without form, and void; and darkness was
upon the face of the deep.

And the Spirit of God moved upon the face of the waters.

And God said, Let there be light; and there was light.

And God said, Let there be a firmament in the midst of the
waters, and let it divide the waters from the waters.

And God said, Let the earth bring forth grass, the herb yielding seed, and the fruit tree yielding fruit

After his kind, whose seed is in itself, upon the earth; and it
was so.

And the earth brought forth grass, and herb yielding seed
after his kind, and the tree yielding fruit,

Whose seed was in itself, after his kind: and God saw that it
was good.

And God said, Let the waters bring forth abundantly the
moving creature that hath life,

And fowl that may fly above the earth in the open firmament of heaven.

And God blessed them, saying, Be fruitful, and multiply, and fill the waters in the seas, and let fowl multiply in the earth.

And God said, Let the earth bring forth the living creature after his kind,

Cattle, and creeping thing, and beast of the earth after his kind: and it was so.

And God made the beast of the earth after his kind, and cattle after their kind,

And everything that creepeth upon the earth after his kind: and God saw that it was good.

And God said, Let us make man in our image, after our likeness:

And let them have dominion over the fish of the sea, and over the fowl of the air,

And over the cattle, and over all the earth, and over every creeping thing that creepeth upon the earth.

So God created man in his own image, in the image of God created he him;

Male and female created he them.

And God blessed them, and God said unto them,

Be fruitful and multiply, and replenish the earth, and subdue it:

And have dominion over the fish of the sea, and over the fowl of the air,

And over every living thing that moveth upon the earth.

And God saw every thing that he had made, and, behold, It was very good.

GENESIS 1

4

. .
.

These are the generations of the heavens and of the earth
when they were created,
In the day that the Lord God made the earth and the heavens,
And every plant of the field before it was in the earth,
And every herb of the field before it grew:

GENESIS 2

. .
.

THE BIBLE WAS WRITTEN
BY HUMAN BEINGS

In studying the Bible we should remember that it was written by
men; men with minds like ours. It is an attempt to set down their
thoughts about God, man, and creation and the relationship between the visible and the invisible.

We shall understand the Bible only when we approach it as a
whole and discover the thread of unified teachings running through
its different texts.

We shall approach our study with the idea in mind that we are
working out a philosophy of life, which deals with man's relationship to Spirit. No attempt will be made to explain all the intricate
sayings of the Bible, but rather to analyze those passages which have
a direct meaning and significance in everyday living.

IN THE BEGINNING

The account of creation, which says that, "in the beginning God created the heaven and the earth," does not refer to a time when there was no creation but rather to the process of eternal creation, which is a continual manifestation of Spirit. An eternal creation is proven by the fact that we must suppose Spirit to be conscious Intelligence, and there can be no conscious intelligence unless it is conscious of something. Spirit is consciousness, hence It must be conscious of something, therefore It must always create.

What a glorious concept is the idea of an eternal creative Principle! There is no stagnation in Spirit, nor should there be any in our idea of spirituality. To be spiritual is to create. The Spirit is alive, conscious, aware, and active *always*.

But how does the Spirit create and from what does It, through Its creative genius, mold definite forms? These questions are pertinent to our philosophy. If we suppose Spirit to be the Life principle running through all things, the cause of all, then we must suppose that It has substance within Itself. It is self-existent consciousness, and also self-existent Substance. Spirit makes things out of Itself through some inner act upon Itself. This inner act must, of course, be an act of consciousness, of self-perception, self-knowingness: What God knows—is.

AND THE EARTH WAS
WITHOUT FORM

"And the earth was without form, and void: and darkness was upon the face of the deep." Prior to creation the creative Substance exists merely as a Divine possibility, a universal stuff, latent with energy and law, ready to receive the Creative Word that shall cause it to spring into definite forms.

That which is visible comes from that which is invisible. This universal, invisible essence, not exactly nothing, yet of itself *no thing*, is susceptible to impressions, ready to take form, and the creative *word* of the Spirit, causes the form to appear through the law of the Spirit, which is an immutable part of Its own nature.

Let us proceed with the account of creation, having this idea in mind; that there is, in the universe, a conscious Intelligence, which we call Spirit; a reactive Law responding to this conscious Intelligence, and a Substance ready to take form through the word of the Spirit. This is the Thing, the way It works, and what It does. Without such a Reality there could be no creation.

AND THE SPIRIT OF GOD MOVED

"And the Spirit of God moved upon the face of the waters." The Spirit of God means the conscious or self-knowing Mind of God; the active principle of conscious selection and self-assertion moving upon the passive principle of creative law, which is called "the waters." (See "The Nature of Being," *The Science of Mind.*) "The waters," as used in the Bible, sometimes means the Law which reacts to the Spirit and at other times refers directly to Spirit Itself.

Next in the account of creation we have the Creative Word used to bring forth a definite manifestation of Itself in concrete form. God is contemplating Himself as creation. This shows that the Spirit has the power of selection and choice. It can create what It chooses; but, of course, It could not choose to create anything that would contradict Its own nature. This is the only limitation of Spirit. It cannot do anything that contradicts Its nature. This is not a real limitation. It is the necessity of Perfection remaining perfect.

A DEFINITE CREATION

"And God said, Let the earth bring forth grass," etc. "Whose seed is in itself, after his kind."

The interesting idea in this passage is, the self-perpetuation of God's thought and the individual definiteness of His concepts. Each creation brings forth after its kind. Back of each manifestation is a definite idea having the power to perpetuate itself. Man evolves from the idea of man, monkey from the idea of monkey. The ideas of Spirit are never confused, the individual manifestations of God are always definite and concrete.

We are next told that God caused manifestations of life to appear in the earth, air, and water, showing the Divine Mind to be omnipresent in Its threefold nature of intelligence, substance, law and action. Energy, life, and intelligence fill all time and space with the representations of Spirit, from the atom to the planet, and in the mineral, vegetable, and animal kingdoms we see vast and endless creations. His lines have gone out in every direction and His Presence encompasses all. And wherever His Presence is, there must be manifestation. Everything is replete with Life.

"And God blessed them," and, "God saw that it was good." It is impossible for the Divine Mind to see other than good or to do other than bless. The curse is self-imposed, through ignorance of the true law of liberty.

THE IMAGE OF GOD

"And God said, Let us make man in our image; after our likeness." "So God created man in his own image, in the image of God created he him; male and female created he them."

God is the One back of all; the Mother-Father Principle back of, in and through everything, the androgynous Unit.

Man is the image of God, reproducing the Divine nature on the scale of the individual life. (See "The Nature of Man," *The Science of Mind.*) Both male and female proceed from the One, who is neither male nor female but who contains the elements of both. (See "Repression and Sublimation," *The Science of Mind.*)

Man is a little world within a big world. God, whose life is self-conscious and whose word is creative, individualizes Himself through man, hence man's life is also self-conscious, and his word becomes creative in his world.

This is the great lesson the Bible sets before us—the creative power of our own thought. In many different ways it approaches the subject, telling what will happen when our thought is constructive, also what will happen when it is destructive. (See "Christ and Antichrist," *The Science of Mind.*) The Bible was written to show the way to freedom under Divine Law.

"And God blessed them, and God said unto them, Be fruitful and multiply . . . and have dominion." The Divine Plan is always one of freedom, God can conceive of nothing less. All bondage, fear, and negation come from a misinterpretation of the Law of Reality.

But the question might be raised, "Why are we created with the possibility of suffering?" This will be answered later under the heading of the story of the Prodigal Son.

INVOLUTION AND EVOLUTION

"These are the generations of the heavens and the earth when they were created. In the day that the Lord God made the earth and the heavens. And every plant of the field, before it was in the earth, and every herb of the field before it grew."

This passage clearly states that before anything was created it already had form in the Divine Mind. Before the herb grew it existed, and before the plants were in the earth they had being. This can have but one meaning which is, that the idea of anything must exist before the fact. This is a teaching of involution and evolution.

Involution is the Divine Creative Word, and evolution runs through everything. Hence we have two accounts of the creation of man. In one we are told that he was made in the image of God, and in the other that he was formed of clay.

Both accounts are true and both are necessary to an understanding of the creative order of the universe. The spiritual man is made in the image of God for he is an intelligent, thinking, knowing center of God-conscious life. This is the first man, made in the image of God. The material man is made of clay, that is, the human body is formed of a stuff common to *all* created things; the ultimate particles of all form are the same. The spiritual man is the idea, the material man is the form; both are necessary since there cannot be an idea without a form or a form without an idea behind it.

THE STORY OF
CREATION SIMPLIFIED

To sum up the account of creation, let us say that someone, generally thought to have been Moses, in expounding his idea of how creation came into being, put his thoughts into the form of a story, giving them to the world shrouded, of course, in symbolic language. Let us state this story in our own words and see what we shall have.

God (meaning the supreme Spirit of the universe) was conscious of Himself before ever this world was created. Being thus conscious of Himself as *all,* and desiring to manifest in form, He did so manifest through the power of His word, which is Law.

God is not only pure Spirit or Intelligence, He is also perfect and immutable Law. God, as pure Spirit, governs the universe through the power of His word. Hence, when He speaks, the Law must obey; the law is mechanical, the word is spontaneous, and God cannot speak a word which contradicts His own nature.

Since God is pure Intelligence and an endless Being, He is always creating something. It is His nature to create, but being all, He must act within Himself. The word of God, spoken within Himself, sets the law, which is also within Himself, in motion. The result is creation. The word is the mold, which, acting through law, produces form; as there are many words, so there are many forms, each distinct and each an individualized idea of God.

Since the word of God is permanent, when He speaks, that word is equipped with the power to perpetuate itself, even as the seed has power within itself to reproduce its kind; it does not become another kind, for this would produce confusion and the Divine Mind is never confused.

God made the mechanical universe, the plant and animal life, but this did not satisfy Him, for He wished to create a being who could respond to and understand Him, hence, He must create a being who has real life within himself. He can do this only by imparting His own nature to this being. He must make him in His own image and likeness. Man must be created out of the stuff of Eternity if he is to have real being. Humanity must partake of the nature of divinity if it is to have real life. So God made man from the highest essence of Himself and clothed this subtle essence with definite form.

And God said within Himself, if I wish to have a man who is a real being I must give him self-choice, he must be spontaneous, not automatic. He must have dominion over everything that is of less intelligence than himself. I will let him name everything that I have created and he shall have all things to enjoy, for his life must be full and complete, if he is to express my nature. So God gave man dominion over all earthly things. Man was not given the power to govern the universe but he *was given* the power to have dominion.

And God, viewing all that He had created, saw that it was good, very good. How could it be otherwise since He had created it; how could God, being goodness, see other than good?

The reader may smile at this rather human narrative and think that it makes God a very finite being, but remember, we are putting into human language a story which can really only be imagined.

Again the evolutionist may say that this is all impossible, because man has come up through the unconscious to the conscious. It is just because man has come up through the unconscious to the conscious that these things can be true. Even God could not make a mechanical individuality. Individuality must ever partake of the nature and essence of spontaneity and self-choice, and can be produced only through evolution. But before anything can evolve it must first be involved. Evolution is the way God works. But to the Divine Mind, time, space, and sequence, cannot be realities; so God must view His work from the beginning as being complete and perfect.

MAN'S SPIRITUAL NATURE

Let us inquire into the meaning of "being made in the image and after the likeness of God?" Surely the writer could not have been speaking of any physical likeness. God is not a huge man, nor is He a finite being circumscribed by limited form. God is Universal Spirit, the Life Principle, and intelligent Energy pervading all. The writer must have been referring to a spiritual and mental likeness, not to a physical correspondence.

Man, as the image of eternity, is made of God stuff. He partakes of the Divine Nature. His likeness to "The Ancient of Days" is a spiritual likeness. On the scale of the individual he reproduces the Universal. As God is, in the big world, so man is in the little world—a small circle within an infinite one—the same elements, the same nature, but not all of that nature. Since this is true of man's nature he is compelled, by reason of that nature, to use a creative power in his own life. God's word is the creative impulse, stirring the universal law into action; man's word reproduces the same power in a smaller way. Man is the creative center of his own individual world. And this within the order of universal law, for man cannot break nor mar the face of eternity.

Let us ponder deeply on this thought. We are creative centers within the whole; individuals equipped with volition and self-choice. What untold agony and what sublime heights this idea supposes!

Heaven or hell, which? As a Man thinketh! Heaven is lost for want of an idea of harmony. Hell is peopled with the symbols of human confusion.

Let us exercise our imagination for a moment and suppose that we are Gods and wish to make man after *our* image and in *our* likeness. We wish him to be free and happy but we know this can be brought about only by creating him and letting him discover his own nature. He must do this through a process of evolution or unfoldment, for could he awake to himself at once he would only awake to an eternal bondage. He must learn by experience, he must evolve through slow processes of time, and gradually become aware of his true nature and his relationship to us. We love him from the start. Indeed our love is so great that we will have nothing short of complete freedom for our creation.

Could we do this unless we made man and let him alone to discover himself? Of course not. As God can do nothing that contradicts His Nature.

Man is made with free will, therefore with the possibility of dual experience. He is not compelled to go one way or the other; but is left to discover which way is best. His thought and act, being creative, become his task master, driving him whither their tendency leads. Do we not recognize in this the law of cause and effect, set in motion through individual volition and free choice. Man can learn only through experience until the time comes when he is in complete unity with God, then he will know without first having experienced.

THE STORY OF THE FALL

This, then, leads us to the story of the Garden of Eden and the Fall.

> And out of the ground made the Lord God to grow every tree that is pleasant to the sight, and good for food; the tree of life also in the midst of the garden, and the tree of the knowledge of good and evil.
>
> And the Lord took the man, and put him into the Garden of Eden to dress it and to keep it.
>
> And the Lord God commanded the man, saying, Of every tree of the garden thou mayest freely eat:
>
> But of the tree of the knowledge of good and evil, thou shalt not eat of it: for in the day that thou eatest thereof thou shalt surely die.

Next in the narrative we have the story of the creation of woman and are told that Adam named everything that lived or had being in his world of experience. Next comes the story of the fall.

> Now the serpent was more subtle than any beast of the field which the Lord God had made. And he said unto the woman, Yea hath God said Ye shall not eat of every tree of the garden?
>
> And the woman said unto the serpent, We may eat of the fruit of the trees of the garden:
>
> But of the fruit of the tree which is in the midst of the garden, God hath said, Ye shall not eat of it, neither shall ye touch it, lest ye die.
>
> And the serpent said unto the woman, Ye shall not surely die:

for God doth know that in the day ye eat thereof, then your eyes shall be opened, and ye shall be as gods, knowing good and evil.

And when the woman saw that the tree was good for food, and that it was pleasant to the eyes, and a tree to be desired to make one wise, she took of the fruit thereof, and did eat, and gave also unto her husband with her; and he did eat.

And the eyes of them both were opened, and they knew that they were naked:

And they heard the voice of the Lord God walking in the garden in the cool of the day: and Adam and his wife hid themselves from the presence of the Lord God, amongst the trees of the garden.

And the Lord God called unto Adam, and said unto him, Where art thou?

And he said, I heard Thy voice in the garden, and I was afraid, because I was naked: and I hid myself.

And he said, Who told thee that thou wast naked? Hast thou eaten of the tree, whereof I commanded thee that thou shouldest not eat?

And the man said, The woman whom thou gavest to be with me, she gave me of the tree, and I did eat.

And the Lord God said unto the woman, What is this that thou hast done? And the woman said, And the serpent beguiled me, and I did eat.

And the Lord God said, Behold, the man is become as one of us, to know good and evil: and now, lest he put forth his hand, and take also of the tree of life, and eat, and live forever: I will send him forth from the garden of Eden.

Here closes the essential part of the story.

THE MEANING OF THE STORY

This story taken literally would be so ridiculous as to be positively absurd; hence, it is necessary to look for a deeper meaning. The writer was trying to teach a Cosmic lesson. He was attempting to teach the lesson of right and wrong.

The Garden of Eden typifies life in its pure essence. Adam means man in general—generic man. Man exists in pure life and has all of its agencies at his command. This is the meaning of his being told to till the soil and enjoy the fruits of his labor.

The tree of life is our real being and the tree of the knowledge of good and evil means the possibility of dual choice—that is, we can choose even that which is not for our best good. Man is warned not to eat of the fruit of this tree for it is destructive.

Eve, the woman in the case, was made from a rib of Adam. This story suggests the dual nature of man as a psychological being. The woman is made from the man. She must have been in him else she could not have been made out of him and the story clearly states that she was taken from his being.

Adam and Eve are potential in all of us. The serpent represents the Life Principle viewed from a material basis and beguiles us in this way; he says that evil is as real as good; that the devil has equal power with God; that negation equals positive goodness and that the universe is dual in its nature. From the acceptance of this argument we experience both good and evil. And should we come full orbed into individuality without having learned the lesson of unity we should live forever in a state of bondage. This is the meaning of God saying, "he shall become as one of us and live forever." The eternal Mind does not wish us to live forever in bondage and this is what would happen unless we first learn the lesson of right and wrong.

And so that part of us which can be fooled eats of the fruit of dual experience and in so doing reveals its own nakedness. The native state of man is one of purity, peace, and perfection, and it is only when he can compare these with impurity, distress, and imperfection, that he is revealed as naked. Emerson tells us that virtue does not know it is virtuous. It is only when virtue tastes of impurities that it becomes naked and must hide from itself.

The voice of God, walking in the Garden in the cool of the day, means the introspective and meditative part of us, which, in its moments of pure intuition and reason, sees the illusion of a life apart from God or Good.

Error is ever a coward before Truth, and cannot hide itself from Reality, which sees through everything, encompasses all and penetrates even the prison walls of the mind with Its clear effulgence.

The conversation between God and Adam and Eve in the Garden of Eden represents the arguments that go on in our own minds when we try to realize the truth. These arguments are familiar to all and need not be enumerated.

The expulsion from the Garden is a necessary and logical outcome of tasting of dual experience. If we believe in both good and evil we must experience both.

THE MISSION OF THE BIBLE

The mission of the Bible is to teach the lesson of life, of individuality and the relationship of the individual to the universal. This it does by showing that God is the Unit back of, in and through all things. A God who is perfect, but a God who works through law. The law must be perfect, but it must also be entirely impersonal.

God, being the essence of Goodness, can never be or do evil, but man, being finite, or undeveloped, does both good and evil, and through experience learns the lesson that good alone is ultimate and absolute.

The law responds to all thought, be it what we call good or evil, for it is and must ever remain a neutral and impersonal force. It then is a doer and not a knower. This is true of all the laws of nature. Man brings upon himself dire calamity, through a misuse of the law, which is the result of ignorance.

The Bible sets before us two grand principles of being: the Law, which is impersonal, and the Spirit, which is personal. When we obey the Spirit we can only do or think good, and good alone can follow; when we wander away and do evil, the Law, which is neither good nor evil—but is simply law—must bring upon us the logical result of our thoughts and acts.

The Bible posits the creative power of thought in man as a necessary complement of the Spirit, in whose spiritual and mental likeness we are made. In a thousand ways the Bible points to the proper and the improper way to contact life.

In parable, in simile, in metaphor and story it points the true way to liberty and freedom. Man is made in the likeness of God, his thought and act is creative, he must reap as he sows—cause and effect; cause and effect.

The Bible starts with Adam as a type of man and ends with Christ as another type; two possibilities latent in all men. In Adam we die and in Christ we live. Adam and Christ are not two people but merely representations of the dual possibility potential in all.

Let us consider what would happen should all men gain a knowledge of the impersonal law, without first having a clear insight into the pure essence of goodness, which is Spirit—we would have a conflict of will and purpose which could only result in disaster; a confusion which must result in chaos. And this brings us to the story of the flood.

The story of the deluge was written to point to the fact that unless humanity be governed by the spirit of goodness its acts become more dangerous as its knowledge expands. What would happen to the world should each individual come to a complete understanding of the mental law without understanding the Spirit back of the law? The inevitable result would be the deluge. The very psychic forces set in motion by the power of the thought of the world would destroy it. In this way we are warned against any infringement of the spirit of the law.

The story of the tower of Babel points to the same lesson; the impossibility of working apart from the Divine Mind. Always confusion results from such an attempt.

While there are many other interesting lessons to be found between the story of creation, and the announcement of the law as given by Moses, both time and space forbid their introduction in a book such as this. We should remember that the mystery of the Bible is no longer necessary. It is a constant repetition of itself and in this age needs only to be read to clearly see the way to the Life and the Truth.

Let us now turn to the teaching of Moses, the great law giver.

· ·
·

Hear, O Israel: The Lord our God is one Lord:
And thou shalt love the Lord thy God with all thine heart,
    and with all thy soul, and with all thy might.
And these words, which I command thee this day, shall be in
    thine heart:
And thou shalt teach them diligently unto thy children, and
    shalt talk of them when thou sittest in thine house,

And when thou walkest by the way, and when thou liest
down, and when thou risest up.

And thou shalt bind them for a sign upon thine hand, and
they shall be as frontlets between thine eyes.

And thou shalt write them upon the posts of thy house, and
on thy gates.

Thou shalt fear the Lord thy God, and serve him, and shalt
swear by his name.

Ye shall not go after other gods, of the gods of the people
which are round about you;

And thou shalt do that which is right and good in the sight of
the Lord:

That it may be well with thee, and that thou mayest go in and
possess the good land which the Lord sware unto thy
fathers.

DEUTERONOMY 6

. .
.

. . . man doth not live by bread only, but by every word
that proceedeth out of the mouth of the Lord doth man
live.

When thou hast eaten and art full, then thou shalt bless the
Lord thy God for the good land which he hath given thee.

Beware that thou forget not the Lord thy God, . . .

Lest when thou hast eaten and art full, and hast built goodly
houses, and dwelt therein;

And when thy herds and thy flocks multiply, and thy silver
and thy gold is multiplied,

And all that thou hast is multiplied;

Then thine heart be lifted up, and thou forget the Lord thy
God, . . .

And thou say in thine heart, My power and the might of mine
hand hath gotten me this wealth.

But thou shalt remember the Lord thy God: for it is he that
giveth thee power to get wealth.

DEUTERONOMY 8

· ·
·

Take heed to yourselves, that your heart be not deceived,

And ye turn aside, and serve other gods, and worship them;

Therefore shall ye lay up these my words in your heart and in
your soul,

And bind them for a sign upon your hand, that they may be as
frontlets between your eyes.

And ye shall teach them unto your children, speaking of
them when thou sittest in thine house,

And when thou walkest by the way, when thou liest down,
and when thou risest up.

And thou shalt write them upon the door posts of thine
house, and upon thy gates:

Every place whereon the soles of your feet shall tread shall
be yours:

Behold, I set before you this day a blessing and a curse;

A blessing, if ye obey the commandments of the Lord your
God, which I command you this day:

And a curse, if ye will not obey the commandments of the
Lord your God,

But turn aside out of the way which I command you this day,

To go after other gods, which ye have not known.

DEUTERONOMY 11

· ·
·

And all these blessings shall come on thee, and overtake thee,

If thou shalt hearken unto the voice of the Lord thy God.

Blessed shalt thou be in the city, and blessed shalt thou be in the field.

Blessed shall be the fruit of thy body, and the fruit of thy ground,

And the fruit of thy cattle, the increase of thy kind, and the flocks of thy sheep.

Blessed shall be thy basket and thy store.

Blessed shalt thou be when thou comest in, and blessed shalt thou be when thou goest out.

DEUTERONOMY 28

For this commandment which I command thee this day, it is not hidden from thee,

Neither is it far off.

It is not in heaven, that thou shouldest say, Who shall go up for us to heaven, and bring it unto us.

That we may hear it, and do it?

Neither is it beyond the sea, that thou shouldest say,

Who shall go over the sea for us, and bring it unto us, that we may hear it, and do it?

But the word is very nigh unto thee, in thy mouth, and in thy heart, that thou mayest do it.

That thou mayest love the Lord thy God, and that thou mayest obey his voice,

And that thou mayest cleave unto him: for he is thy life, and the length of thy days:

DEUTERONOMY 30

. .
.

Be strong and of good courage, fear not, nor be afraid . . .

For the Lord thy God, he it is that doth go with thee; he will
not fail thee, nor forsake thee.

And the Lord, he it is that doth go before thee; he will be
with thee,

He will not fail thee, neither forsake thee; fear not, neither
be dismayed.

DEUTERONOMY 31

. .
.

Give ear, O ye heavens, and I will speak; and hear, O earth,
the words of my mouth.

My doctrine shall drop as the rain, my speech shall distil as
the dew,

As the small rain upon the tender herb, and as the showers
upon the grass:

Because I will publish the name of the Lord: ascribe ye great-
ness unto our God.

He is the Rock, his work is perfect: for all his ways are judgment:

A God of truth and without iniquity, just and right is he.

DEUTERONOMY 32

. .
.

The eternal God is thy refuge, and underneath are the everlasting arms: . . .

DEUTERONOMY 33

. .
.

From the Teachings of Moses
the Great Lawgiver

Moses was the great lawgiver and today our code of laws is based largely upon principles which he announced. This because he taught a universal law, an eternal verity which remains the same, yesterday, today and forever. Moses taught the universal law of cause and effect, an eye for an eye and a tooth for a tooth. It remained for Jesus to teach a God of love and understanding. The teachings of Jesus complete those of Moses; taken together, they reveal the universal presence of Love and the universal necessity of Law.

In the twentieth chapter of Exodus we find the law of Moses given in a concise manner. These laws are fundamental and need no defining other than to remark how completely they are based upon the idea of God as a present reality. In the twenty-third chapter we find a statement that God will heal disease when we trust in His presence; and in the twenty-sixth chapter of Leviticus we find these words, "And I will set my tabernacle among you . . . and I will walk among you, and will be your God, and ye shall be my people."

THE DIVINE PRESENCE

If there is anything necessary to an individual sense of security, peace of mind, and satisfaction of soul it is, greater than all else, a sense of the Divine Presence, a realization that there is a power which knows, cares, and understands. Without this sense of security we feel lost. It makes no difference how loudly the materialist may shout or in what language he speaks; the merely intellectual may disclaim all divine revelation and spiritual guidance; but to the pure in heart and to the childlike mind there will forever be vouchsafed this sense of certainty. This is not an illusion, nor is it an intellectual weakness; it is a spiritual experience. And just as we have physical experiences so we may have spiritual ones.

Moses sensed the Divine Presence and must have lived very close to it. In the sixth chapter of Deuteronomy, "Hear, O Israel: The Lord our God is one Lord." Here is a perception of the Unity of Good, a realization of the One Life running through all. God is One, this is the teaching of Moses. We are to love this One with all our heart and with all our soul and with all our might. That is, we are to completely surrender ourselves to the realization of the Unity of Good—the presence of God. We are to trust this God and rely solely upon His presence in every experience.

We are to so completely sense this Presence that the heart will respond and the emotions acquiesce. Without such an emotional agreement, words are empty and ideas void of real meaning. Emerson tells us that when this divine moment comes we are to leave everything else and flee into its loving embrace.

Moses tells us that we are to teach the knowledge of God to our children and to talk about God when we sit in our houses and when we walk by the way. We are to see the evidence of Spirit manifested in everything. The God of the living, who lives in all and through all. We are not to go after other gods as do those who have not put their trust in Good alone, but we are to trust and not be afraid.

In the seventh chapter of the same book we are told that God will bless and multiply our benefits if we keep His laws. Moses enumerates the different ways in which this blessing will be made manifest—in all that we do. Jesus, speaking many years later, tells the same story when he says to seek the Kingdom first and other things will be added. How true this teaching is. The greater always includes the lesser and all the lessers must be included in the Infinite Mind.

In the eighth chapter of Deuteronomy we are warned against thinking that we can, of ourselves and without Divine aid, accomplish. In the day of accomplishment we are not to forget that we are beneficiaries of Life. How soon must that light be extinguished which is no longer connected with the center of energy! This is a universal truth and should be heeded.

We are not to suppose that God is jealous but we are to realize that unity is unity. We live on three planes simultaneously, spirit, soul, and body, and our thought and belief decide what is to happen to us. It makes all the difference in the world where we place our trust and faith. God is not jealous, but the law is One and cannot be divided.

THE BLESSING AND THE CURSE

In the eleventh chapter of Deuteronomy we find these words, "Behold, I set before you this day a blessing and a curse; a blessing, if ye obey the commandments . . . and a curse, if ye will not obey the commandments." From a superficial reading it looks as though God blesses us when we please Him but will curse us if we displease Him. This, however, is not the meaning of the passage. God neither blesses nor curses. God is always God, always Good, always Goodness. But God is always Law and the law must forever remain neutral and impersonal. If we contact it in mercy, it will show mercy, if we contact it in judgment it will judge. The law responds and corresponds to our attitudes and actions. Every law of nature is either a blessing or a curse according to the way in which it is contacted.

Moses is repeating himself. He is telling the story of Eden in another way. He is again pointing to the fact of individuality, which is free choice, and the law which is retroactive. The statement could not be put more plainly. Life returns to the thinker that which he thinks.

Jesus says that those who live by the sword shall perish by it; that it is done unto us as we believe. Moses is saying the same thing, is teaching the same lesson. We must accept life—either as good or as evil. We must worship life in the symbolic form of God or the devil. Heaven and hell are ideas in our own minds, peopled with our own thoughts. The man who loves will *be* loved, the man who hates cannot be happy. Automatically the law becomes a thing of freedom or a taskmaster of bondage.

There is no apartness from the Spirit and when one is assumed only sorrow and grief can follow. God Is, and the sooner we realize this truth the better for ourselves. In no way can we disrupt the harmony of the Divine Being, but we do disrupt our own harmony when we are out of line with Truth.

Life is always a blessing or a curse, according to the way we contact it. The choice is up to the individual who, alone, is responsible—to himself—for his own thoughts and acts.

The twenty-eighth chapter of Deuteronomy is one filled with blessings—the good that naturally follows those who live in accord with divine law. We are told that blessings shall overtake us on the way; that we shall be blessed when we go in and when we come out, and that all the works of our hands shall be blessed. Here is hope, reason and justification for our faith, for "faith without works is dead."

THE WORD IS IN
OUR OWN MOUTH

And in Deuteronomy the thirtieth chapter we are told that the word of power is not afar off but in our own mouths that we may know and do it. Here, again, Moses is bringing the burden of proof home to the individual life. Life is from within out, never from without in. The word is in our own mouth. The word is our own being. The word is our belief in Life and when that word is one with Life it IS Life.

Again we find a parallel between the teachings of Jesus and Moses. Moses tells us that the word is in our own mouth, and Jesus, that the Kingdom of Heaven is within. Language cannot state a proposition more clearly. The issues of life are from within. The Creative Spirit has imparted Its own life to us. We are made from Life and we are Life. The great teacher said, "I am the Way, the Truth and the Life." And all men are alike.

The blessing or the curse is in our own mouth. What responsibility and what opportunity! What vistas of divine possibility lie hidden in the human soul! Eye has not seen, ear has not heard but the still small voice has proclaimed, "Man, know thyself." And, "the eternal God is thy refuge, and underneath are the everlasting arms."

READINGS FROM THE NEW TESTAMENT

From the Teachings of Jesus

It is written, Man shall not live by bread alone,
But by every word that proceedeth out of the mouth of God.
Thou shalt worship the Lord thy God, and him only shalt
thou serve.

Matthew 4

• •
•

Blessed are the poor in spirit: for theirs is the kingdom of
heaven.
Blessed are they that mourn; for they shall be comforted.
Blessed are the meek: for they shall inherit the earth.
Blessed are they which do hunger and thirst after righteous-
ness: for they shall be filled.
Blessed are the merciful: for they shall obtain mercy.
Blessed are the pure in heart: for they shall see God.
Blessed are the peacemakers: for they shall be called the chil-
dren of God.

Ye are the light of the world. A city that is set on an hill cannot be hid.

Let your light so shine before men, that they may see your good works,

And glorify your Father which is in heaven.

Therefore, if thou bring thy gift to the altar, and there rememberest that thy brother hath aught against thee;

Leave there thy gift before the altar, and go thy way; first be reconciled to thy brother, and then come and offer thy gift.

Agree with thine adversary quickly, whiles thou art in the way with him; lest at any time the adversary deliver thee to the judge.

And the judge deliver thee to the officer, and thou be cast into prison.

Verily I say unto thee, Thou shalt by no means come out thence, till thou hast paid the uttermost farthing.

Ye have heard that it hath been said, An eye for an eye, and a tooth for a tooth.

But I say unto you, That ye resist not evil;

Give to him that asketh thee, and from him that would borrow of thee turn not thou away.

Ye have heard that it hath been said, Thou shalt love thy neighbour, and hate thine enemy:

But I say unto you, Love your enemies, bless them that curse you, do good to them that hate you,

And pray for them which despitefully use you, and persecute you;

That ye may be the children of your Father which is in heaven:

For he maketh his sun to rise on the evil and on the good, and sendeth rain on the just and on the unjust.

For if ye love them which love you, what reward have ye? do not even the publicans the same?

And if ye salute your brethren only, what do ye more than others? do not even the publicans so?

Be ye therefore perfect, even as your Father which is in heaven is perfect.

MATTHEW 5

WHY JESUS HAD SUCH POWER

No attempt is made to explain all the sayings of Jesus. He lived in a world of spiritual realizations far beyond that of which the average man has any understanding; and as spiritual things must be spiritually understood, so the full meaning of his sayings can never be clear to us until we have attained a consciousness equal to his. But in the record of his sayings there is much which bears witness to our own belief, and no doubt, could we penetrate completely into the meaning of his teaching, we should have a perfect explanation of our own philosophy.

Jesus discerned spiritual truth. Why or how, we do not know, nor does it make any difference. That he did understand life was witnessed by his words and through his works. The world has not produced another like him and until it does he must receive a unique place in the history of human character.

We should not look upon him as being different from other men except in understanding and spiritual enlightenment. The simplest explanation of his power is the most direct and the truest. Jesus understood spiritual things because he specialized in them. His life was given over to the study of God, man, and the universe and the relationship between the creature and the Creator. With a mind trained to clear thinking, a spirit open and receptive to divine revelation, and with a childlike faith in the presence of God, he lived as though what he taught was true.

MAN SHALL NOT LIVE BY BREAD ALONE

What did he teach? "It is written that man shall not live by bread alone, but by every word that proceedeth out of the mouth of God." "Thou shalt worship the Lord thy God, and him only shalt thou serve."

This is a repetition of the teaching of Moses whose whole thought centered around the same theme. God is One. Man is the product of this One and comes to himself only as he approaches the One. Man lives *by* and *through* the One, ever and always.

Who eats of bread alone, even though he add meat and vegetables, will continually hunger. To the physical benefits of the human board must be added the spiritual strength of divine wisdom. The poor in spirit receive the kingdom of heaven before the proud and arrogant. And how rich is this kingdom compared to human possessions! The mourners shall be comforted and the tears of sorrow wiped away by the realization of God's presence when their thought is upward bent and their eyes toward heaven.

THE MEEK SHALL INHERIT
THE EARTH

"The meek shall inherit the earth." This is a teaching of nonresistance. War lords and plunderers of human possessions have come and gone. Kingdoms have risen only to crumble in dust and become numbered with past events. Passion and lust for power have strewn the earth with destruction; it would seem as though the meek had lost out in the titanic struggle for temporal supremacy.

In the midst of this drama of human existence, Jesus declared that the meek shall inherit the earth. Let us inquire if his teaching was a true one. Do we teach our children to follow the steps of a Cæsar and a Napoleon? Or do we tell them the story of Jesus or Buddha. The cross is mightier than the crown and we teach our children that love masters everything. The meek shall inherit the earth. To whom have our artists turned for inspiration and that quickening power which enables them to depict the ideal? Not to the war lords nor even the captains of industry—but to the meek. What characteristics are set before us as being worthy? Have not faith and belief in the divine Goodness been the theme of our greatest singers. Who could write a beautiful story about hell? But heaven and love have inspired thousands to the uplifting of humanity. Jesus was right when he said that the meek shall inherit the earth. They have done so and will continue so to do.

THEY THAT HUNGER SHALL BE FED

"They who hunger and thirst after righteousness shall be filled." Is there anyone who does not have a soul hunger? Does not the spirit of man thirst after knowledge and understanding? The old Cosmic Urge is behind all this. Man has more within him than he dreams— and yet he does dream of that fairer land—he yearns for truth and reality, as blind men yearn for light. And his hunger can only be satisfied with spiritual food—as manna from heaven.

Let us inquire into this teaching and see if it be an illusion. Turn to the history of those who have been spiritually minded and the question is answered. All who have been hungry have been fed, their hunger has been blessed in that it has led them to that only food, that heavenly manna, which has sustained, strengthened, and upheld them while the rest of the world has eagerly inquired from what store they bought their goods. They who hunger and thirst after Reality are always fed, and directly, by the hand of God Himself.

THE MERCIFUL SHALL
OBTAIN MERCY

"Blessed are the merciful: for they shall obtain mercy." Again we are confronted with an apparent contradiction. Do the merciful always obtain mercy? From casual observation it would seem otherwise. But are not many of our observations based on a limited concept, from a finite outlook? Can we estimate life from the range of one human experience? If life begins with the cradle and ends with the grave, then are all our hopes, not only forlorn, but useless. It is only when the "Eye views the world as one vast plain, one boundless reach of sky," that it sees truly.

The perspective of reality is lost when we view life from the range of a short experience. Jesus saw beyond the veil and estimated life from the great perspective—the long run of the adventure of the soul. He knew that the law of cause and effect takes care of all and that the "Mills of God" will grind the chaff of unreality from the wheat of the spirit. What matter if these mills do not do all their grinding while we are clothed in flesh! Did not Jesus know of another life which to him was as real as this one? Can we expect, in this world, to receive full compensation for all our work? Of course not. We are building on an eternal foundation, one that time cannot alter nor experience destroy.

A true estimate of real values cannot be built on the shifting sands of time alone. In the long run the merciful will obtain mercy. In the long run we shall reap as we have sown.

THE PURE IN HEART
SHALL SEE GOD

"The pure in heart shall see God." Can we ever see God? Is there any news of Heaven other than that which comes through our own thought or, through the thought of another? Who thinks purity sees it, and is beholding God. The face of "The Ancient of Days" onlooks eternity and the upward glance ever sees this reality in all things. The pure in heart not only *shall* see, but *do* see God.

The peacemakers are called the children of God. We never associate warriors with the divine kingdom. Struggle and strife are outside the kingdom, they cannot enter in because of their confusion. Only peace can enter the gates of reality and sit at the table of love. The Divine Host serves not his bounty to confusion, but distributes his gifts to those who enter his gates with peace in their minds, and love in their hearts.

"Ye are the light of the world." Man is the candle of the Lord. Is there anywhere else in this world where the light of the Lord shines so clearly as through the mind of man? The mind of man is the only self-knowing and consciously directive creation that we know.

It is necessary that the mind of man become the light of the world, for it is only through this avenue that truth can come to us. How important, then, that this light be kept trimmed and burning, with the oil of pure spirit through the wick of peace and joy. In this way do we glorify that Indwelling God who is the Heavenly Father and the Cosmic Mother of all.

THE ALTAR OF FAITH

Again, Jesus tells us that our gifts, brought to the altar of life, are unacceptable while there is aught between us and our fellow man. Here is a hard saying. We cannot always please our fellow men. Human experience has taught that this is impossible. What attitude, then, are we to assume? This, whether we please, or, whether we displease, we need have no personal animosity toward others; we can keep any thoughts of other's hatred toward us away by refusing to recognize it.

The altar of faith is approached only through peace and good will toward all. We cannot disrupt heaven by our tales of woe. The

Divine Ear is attuned to harmony alone and cannot be approached through discord.

When we agree with our adversaries quickly, we shall cease to recognize them as adversaries and they will disappear as such. There can be no reality to us, unless we recognize it. But if we recognize that which is false, giving it life and apparent being by our acceptance of it, we shall be delivered to the judgment whereby we have, ourselves, judged, and the utmost farthing must be paid until we see no error and no longer indulge in it.

Jesus tells us to resist not evil, to love our enemies, and do good to them who would do us evil, for this is to manifest the spirit of love, which is God. God loves all alike and causes His rain and sun to come alike to all. Divine love encompasses everything, in arms which are all inclusive.

. .
.

Take heed that ye do not your alms before men, to be seen of
    them;
Otherwise ye have no reward of your Father which is in
    heaven.
Therefore, when thou doest thine alms, do not sound a trum-
    pet before thee, as the hypocrites do in the synagogues
    and in the streets, that they may have glory of men.
Verily I say unto you. They have their reward.
But when thou doest alms, let not thy left hand know what
    thy right hand doeth;
That thine alms may be in secret: and thy Father which seeth
    in secret himself shall reward thee openly.
And when thou prayest, thou shalt not be as the hypocrites
    are: for they love to pray standing in the synagogues

and in the corners of the streets, that they may be seen of men.

Verily I say unto you, They have their reward.

But thou, when thou prayest, enter into thy closet, and when thou hast shut thy door, pray to thy Father which is in secret; and thy Father which seeth in secret shall reward thee openly.

But when ye pray, use not vain repetitions, as the heathen do: for they think that they shall be heard for their much speaking.

Be not ye therefore like unto them: for your Father knoweth what things ye have need of before ye ask him.

After this manner therefore pray ye:

Our Father which art in heaven, Hallowed be thy name.

Thy kingdom come. Thy will be done in earth, as it is in heaven.

Give us this day our daily bread. And forgive us our debts, as we forgive our debtors.

And lead us not into temptation, but deliver us from evil:

For thine is the kingdom, and the power, and the glory, for ever. Amen.

For if ye forgive men their trespasses, your heavenly Father will also forgive you: But if ye forgive not men their trespasses, neither will your Father forgive your trespasses.

Moreover, when ye fast, be not, as the hypocrites, of a sad countenance: for they disfigure their faces, that they may appear unto men to fast.

Verily I say unto you, They have their reward.

But thou, when thou fastest, anoint thine head, and wash thy face; That thou appear not unto men to fast, but unto thy

Father which is in secret: and Thy Father, which seeth in secret, shall reward thee openly.

Lay not up for yourselves treasures upon earth, where moth and rust doth corrupt, and where thieves break through and steal:

But lay up for yourselves treasures in heaven, where neither moth nor rust doth corrupt, and where thieves do not break through nor steal:

For where your treasure is, there will your heart be also.

The light of the body is the eye: if therefore thine eye be single, thy whole body shall be full of light.

But if thine eye be evil, thy whole body shall be full of darkness. If therefore the light that is in thee be darkness, how great is that darkness!

No man can serve two masters: for either he will hate the one, and love the other; or else he will hold to the one, and despise the other. Ye cannot serve God and mammon.

Therefore I say unto you, Take no thought for your life, what ye shall eat, or what ye shall drink; nor yet for your body, what ye shall put on. Is not the life more than meat, and the body than raiment?

Behold the fowls of the air: for they sow not, neither do they reap, nor gather into barns; yet your heavenly Father feedeth them. Are ye not much better than they?

Which of you, by taking thought, can add one cubit unto his stature?

And why take ye thought for raiment? Consider the lilies of the field, how they grow: they toil not, neither do they spin: and yet I say unto you, That even Solomon in all his glory was not arrayed like one of these.

Wherefore, if God so clothe the grass of the field, which
today is, and tomorrow is cast into the oven, shall he not
much more clothe you, O ye of little faith?

Therefore take no thought, saying, What shall we eat? or,
What shall we drink? or, Where-withal shall we be
clothed? (For after all these things do the Gentiles seek:)
for your heavenly Father knoweth that ye have need of all
these things.

But seek ye first the kingdom of God, and his righteousness;
and all these things shall be added unto you.

Take therefore no thought for the morrow: for the morrow
shall take thought for the things of itself. Sufficient unto
the day is the evil thereof.

MATTHEW 6

THE FATHER WHO SEETH
IN SECRET

We are not to give our alms before men to be seen of them, but to
do good for the pure love of good. Here Jesus is teaching the lesson
of sincerity. We must be free from all hypocrisy and pretense; live a
straightforward and unassuming life, free from any attempt to be
thought great. Men will come and men will go, friend and foe alike
may fall away but—always the soul shall be thrown back upon itself. The indwelling Spirit who lives in the secret place of our lives
will ever be with us. And this Father who seeth in secret will reward us openly. Here, again, is a suggestion of the law of cause and
effect which Jesus tells us so much about.

Our prayers are to be made to God in the secret place of our own being. They are not to be shouted aloud for the ears of men. The soul must enter this secret place, naked and alone. This is how the One returns to the One.

THE SECRET OF PRAYER

The secret of prayer and its power in the outward life depends upon an unconditioned faith in, and reliance upon, this inner presence. We must enter the closet. That is, we are to shut out all else and enter the precinct of Spirit in quietness and confidence—believing. Prayer has power, not through repetition but by belief and acceptance. Prayer is to be simple, direct and receiving. We are to believe that God indwells our own life, that this Divine Presence is sufficient for all needs. We are to believe that God will provide for and bless us abundantly. And when we enter this secret place we are to leave all else behind; all hate, animosity, and vindictiveness. We are to forgive and forget all that cannot enter heaven, for only in so doing can *we* enter.

HOW GOD FORGIVES

We are told that God will forgive us after we have first forgiven others. This is a direct statement and one that we should ponder deeply. Can God forgive until we have forgiven? If God can work for us only by working through us, then this statement of Jesus stands true and is really a statement of the law of cause and effect.

We cannot afford to hold personal animosities or enmities against the world or individual members of society. All such thoughts are outside the law and cannot be taken into the heavenly consciousness. Love alone can beget love. People do not gather roses from thistles.

The Father who seest in secret will reward us openly. Shall we not learn to enter the "secret place of the most High" within our own soul in gladness? We are to fast without outward sign but with the inner mind open and receptive to the Good, alone. Our treasure is already in heaven and our thought can take us to this treasure only when it is in accord with divine harmony and perfect love.

THE SINGLE EYE

If our eye is single we shall be filled with light. That is, when we perceive the Unity of Good we shall perceive it in its entirety, an undivided whole. But if our eye be filled with evil we shall remain in darkness. We must cleave to the good and trust absolutely in the law of God to bring about any desired end. The Divine Mind will mold our purposes when we allow It to do so. As we learn to depend more and more upon the perfect law we shall find that the outward things which are necessary to our good, will be provided. We shall be cared for as the lilies of the field, which live directly upon the Divine bounty. And yet they toil not nor do they spin.

THE DIVINE BOUNTY

As God cares for the birds who do not gather into barns, so shall we be cared for if we trust and do not doubt. But we are to seek the Kingdom first. Jesus bids us to completely trust in God for everything and in every instance. He had a complete reliance upon God. Dare we say that such a confidence will be misplaced? Have we ever tried it? Until we have tried and failed we are not in a position to contradict this theory. Those who have are proving the principle to be definite and one upon which an absolute reliance may be placed.

Have no fear of tomorrow; enjoy today. Refuse to carry the corpse of a mistaken yesterday. What untold misery is suffered through the burdens imposed by our yesterdays and the bitter prospects of our tomorrows! The good of the present day is too often sandwiched between these two impossible situations. The day in which we live is sufficient. We are to live today as though God were in His Heaven while all is well with our souls.

Jesus made the greatest claim upon God, of anyone who ever lived. He demands a complete and unreserved trust in the goodness and loving kindness of the Creator. And harking down the ages—since he lived and taught his marvelous philosophy to mankind, those who have followed his teaching have been justified in their faith.

. .
.

Judge not, that ye be not judged. For with what judgment ye
judge, ye shall be judged: and with what measure ye
mete, it shall be measured to you again.

And why beholdest thou the mote that is in thy brother's eye, but considerest not the beam that is in thine own eye?

Or how wilt thou say to thy brother, Let me pull out the mote out of thine eye; and, behold, a beam is in thine own eye?

Thou hypocrite, first cast out the beam out of thine own eye; and then shalt thou see clearly to cast out the mote out of thy brother's eye.

Give not that which is holy unto the dogs, neither cast ye your pearls before swine, lest they trample them under their feet, and turn again and rend you.

Ask, and it shall be given you; seek, and ye shall find; knock, and it shall be opened unto you:

For every one that asketh receiveth; and he that seeketh findeth; and to him that knocketh it shall be opened.

Or what man is there of you, whom if his son ask bread, will he give him a stone? Or if he ask a fish, will he give him a serpent?

If ye then, being evil, know how to give good gifts unto your children, how much more shall your Father which is in heaven give good things to them that ask him!

Therefore all things whatsoever ye would that men should do to you, do ye even so to them: for this is the Law and the Prophets.

Enter ye in at the straight gate: for wide is the gate, and broad is the way, that leadeth to destruction, and many there be which go in thereat:

Because straight is the gate, and narrow is the way, which leadeth unto life, and few there be that find it.

Beware of false prophets, which come to you in sheep's clothing, but inwardly they are ravening wolves.

Ye shall know them by their fruits. Do men gather grapes of
thorns, or figs of thistles?

Even so every good tree bringeth forth good fruit; but a corrupt tree bringeth forth evil fruit.

A good tree cannot bring forth evil fruit, neither can a corrupt tree bring forth good fruit.

Every tree that bringeth not forth good fruit is hewn down,
and cast into the fire.

Wherefore by their fruits ye shall know them.

Not every one that saith unto me, Lord, Lord, shall enter
into the kingdom of heaven; but he that doeth the will of
my Father which is in heaven.

Many will say to me in that day, Lord, Lord, have we not
prophesied in thy name? and in thy name have cast out
devils; and in thy name done many wonderful works?

And then will I profess unto them, I never knew you: depart
from me, ye that work iniquity.

Therefore, whosoever heareth these sayings of mine, and
doeth them, I will liken him unto a wise man, which built
his house upon a rock:

And the rain descended, and the floods came, and the winds
blew, and beat upon that house; and it fell not: for it was
founded upon a rock.

And every one that heareth these sayings of mine, and doeth
them not, shall be likened unto a foolish man, which built
his house upon the sand:

And the rain descended, and the floods came, and the winds
blew, and beat upon that house; and it fell: and great was
the fall of it.

And it came to pass, when Jesus had ended these sayings, the
people were astonished at his doctrine:

For he taught them as one having authority, and not as the scribes.

MATTHEW 7

. .
.

"JUDGE NOT, THAT YE BE NOT JUDGED"

"Judge not that ye be not judged, for with what judgment ye judge ye shall be judged, and with what measure ye mete, it shall be measured to you again." This statement could come only from one who had a deep insight into the universal law of cause and effect which balances everything and sees that, in the long run, everyone receives his just due. This law Emerson called the High Chancellor of God. The law of cause and effect is the law of perfect balance, of logical sequence and of inevitable consequence. Whatever a man sows he must reap. If he has sown in ignorance he must reap in like manner.

All great spiritual teachers have announced this law and its inevitable consequence. In the teachings of the East this is known as the Karmic Law. Jesus taught the same law but under another name and with this difference, that through right action—by reversing one's order of thought, desire, and purpose, and thereby establishing an harmonious relationship with the universe—one can transcend, neutralize, or overcome the result of his previous actions. In theology this is known as the remission of sin or Divine forgiveness. It is said that this idea of forgiveness is what caused Saint Augustine to espouse the doctrine of Christianity.

The ethics and morals of Buddhism are as sublime as those of Jesus, but the idea in the Buddhistic philosophy, that man can never transcend or overcome his Karmic Law, naturally produced, in the psychology of the Eastern mind, a state of apathy and inaction, which is a logical result of the belief that one must forever suffer from his previous mistakes. This state of inaction is evident in those who adhere to this philosophy.

TRANSCENDING
ONE'S MISTAKES

The Christian Philosophy, which teaches the possibility of transcending one's mistakes, produces a psychology of optimism and hopefulness which finds its logical correspondent in action, progress, and a more rapid evolution of the individual soul. This spirit is apparent among those who espouse the cause of Christianity.

But the Christian Philosophy clearly teaches that the law of cause and effect is immutable and that every man's action produces an effect in his life which he must ultimately experience unless he transcends the law already set in motion. Such a concept supposes that we are surrounded by a universal law which is entirely impartial and which returns to the thinker the logical effect of his actions. Man, being a free agent in this law, whether consciously or in ignorance, is continuously setting it in motion to some definite end; therefore it is true that he must reap as he has sown.

With the above stated idea in mind, let us analyze the meaning of the saying, "Judge not that ye be not judged, for with what judgment ye judge ye shall be judged; and with what measure ye mete, it shall be measured to you again." This means that life must return to us the manifestation of our motives, thoughts and desires, whether these motives, thoughts and desires were intended for ourselves or otherwise. It means that the thought of judgment, criticism, and condemnation must in time operate against the one who sets it in motion. It is doubtless necessary to the well-being of society that our civil laws be enforced, else in our present state of evolution there would be no protection from those who seek to destroy society, but personal condemnation can be entirely eliminated. People who are filled with personal condemnation have a very limited outlook on life and are greatly to be pitied.

AN EVOLVED SOUL
JUDGES NO ONE

Every soul in its struggle to scale the heights of spiritual perception must, on the way, express itself at the level of its own evolution, its own mental horizon. A careful study of psychology shows that those who continually condemn are either bound by the morbidity and intolerance of a false religion and a narrow philosophy or else they are suffering from an inferiority complex.

Ultimately we shall see that the universe rests on the shoulders of Love, that God is Love, and that all the errors of man are the result of ignorance of his own true nature. The happy outlook on life is always constructive, and the understanding heart is filled with sympathy and helpfulness to all. An evolved soul judges no one, condemns no one, but realizes that all are on the road of experience, seeking the same goal, and that each must ultimately find his home in Heaven.

A PSYCHOLOGICAL EXPERIMENT WITH PLANTS

One of our scientific writers in the realm of spiritual psychology tells of an experiment which some friends of his conducted with two rose bushes. Going out each morning they condemned one and praised the other; saying to one, "You are a miserable, worthless little plant," and to the other, "You are beautiful and growing magnificently," with the result that in a short time the mistreated bush shriveled and died, while the other bloomed and flowered in beauty and abundance. Is it any wonder that Luther Burbank, who so loved his plants, could produce such marvelous effects with them? Is it any wonder that a mother who is continuously condemning her children finds them irritable and hard to manage, while the mother who thinks of her children as being harmonious and happy, is lifting their little souls to the light, thus helping them to reflect the Divine Reality?

THE HOME ATMOSPHERE

Could we know the action of thought, and clearly see its effects, we would never again condemn anyone but would look upon all with love. The wife who keeps her home in an atmosphere of cheer, never allowing herself to be morbid or fearful, will generally find that her husband would swim the ocean, cross the desert or scale the mountain tops to be with her.

If we better understood the action of thought we would understand why it is that the man who says, "The world is against me, no one understands me, no one appreciates me," makes it impossible for good to come to him.

PEOPLE WHO ARE SUCCESSFUL

People who are successful look upon life with radiant expression, with cheerful enthusiasm and receptive minds. They do not say, "Everything is wrong and everyone is against me," they feel that everything is for them. We may hear them say, "Conditions are temporarily wrong but they are straightening out," or, "Things are not just as they should be but everything will come out all right in the end." This does not mean that they are saying things are right when they are wrong; it means that successful people have an inner conviction that things are fundamentally right with the world.

The critical, condemning, judging type have a sour look, a dyspeptic countenance and an unhealthy atmosphere. Healthy, happy, normal people find such mentalities distasteful and shun them; in so doing they act wisely.

In the long run nothing judges us but the immutable law of cause and effect. Whoever deserves punishment will receive it and whoever merits reward will find that it is brought by the hand of the Almighty and delivered to him. There is a direct law responding to condemnation and a direct law responding to praise and appreciation. It is, of course, the same law used in different ways.

CONDEMNATION AND HEALTH

The one whose thought continually rests upon his bodily condition will never be physically well. Nature has intelligently provided for the automatic functions of the body and the less the average person knows about his body, other than that it is harmonious, the healthier his body generally is. This is a fact which can easily be verified by observation. The one who knows little about how his food digests seldom has trouble with digestion. When we realize that digestion *was,* before we were aware of the fact, we shall see that the only thing hindering it is our attitude of condemnation toward it. This is true of every organ in the body. A perfectly well man never wonders whether his heart or any other organ is working correctly, while the average invalid is conscious of everything that is wrong. The invalid should stop condemning his body, indeed, he should forget it entirely and, learning to live in a happy frame of mind, he will soon find that the physical instrument responds and becomes harmonious.

There is a law common to all people which responds to every man's belief in life, at the level of that belief. No man can be happy who lives in a continuous state of condemnation of people, conditions, and things. We must learn to praise and not condemn. We have no right to judge people.

RELIGIOUS MORBIDITIES

Those who have made a thorough study of the analysis of the soul are aware of the fact that poisonous secretions in the body are often the result of religious morbidity; all of these religious morbidities arise from some form of false judgment. The time has come to break the bondage of wrong statements. We are free souls, free spirits, and whatever God is, we are of a like nature, else we could not be. Because this is true our thought has creative power, and since our thought has creative power we must carefully choose what we are to think, for everything moves in circles.

We do not say there is no evil and evil cannot be. We say rather, that evil is not an entity but is a misuse of a power which of itself is perfectly good. We shall never know the nature of good by dissecting the nature of evil.

THOUGHT RETARDS OR QUICKENS

Everything our thought rests upon is either retarded or quickened by the power of that thought. Everyone is a law unto himself under the great law of cause and effect governing all things.

When we constructively praise and creatively bless, life abounds with love, peace, and joy. "There is no god dare wrong a worm." Let goodness shine forth. Let us learn to see in everyone an evolving Christ. Let us so live and think that we may retire at night in peace, knowing that no harm can come to the soul; that we may rise in the morning renewed in body and in mind, with a brighter outlook, a happier expectation, and a clearer joy, looking upon all with love, condemning none, and blessing even those who seek to injure us. Let us learn to be perfect even as that Divine being, residing in the heart of all and overshadowing eternity, must also be perfect.

SELF-HEALING MUST COME FIRST OF ALL

If we think we can guide our brother aright while our own feet still walk in darkness we are mistaken. We must first clarify our own vision, then we shall become as lights lighting the way for others. But can we teach a lesson we have not learned? Can we give that which we do not possess? To suppose so is hypocrisy, a thing to be shunned. Jesus tears the mantle of unreality from the shoulders of hypocrisy, winnowing from the soul of sham and shallowness its last shred of illusion. We cannot see reality until our eyes are open; until the light of eternal Truth has struck deeply into our own souls.

PEARLS AND SWINE

The sacredness of Truth is given value by the teaching that we should not cast pearls before swine. Spiritual truths cannot be taught to those who will not accept them. The wisdom of this world is foolishness to a greater wisdom; and the wisdom of Spirit is often overlooked by human foolishness.

We should not forget that Jesus was an illumined soul; he saw clearly that which we only look for. This is why he spoke as one having authority. Since he was able to prove his wisdom by his works we shall do well to accept his teaching.

SCIENTIFIC PRAYER

We now come to a definite teaching regarding prayer. We shall receive that for which we ask. It shall be opened to us when we knock and we shall find that for which we are searching. This teaching implies the definiteness of spiritual and mental work. God is Intelligent Mind and Spirit, and there is a direct response from this Universal Intelligence to our intelligence. If we ask for bread we *shall not* receive a stone. But we are told that we must ask, *believing,* if we are to receive.

Here again we are meeting the law of cause and effect in the teachings of Jesus. Prayer is a mental as well as a spiritual function of intelligence. It is a certain manner of approach to the Spirit, a conscious act of the mind, a concrete experience of the knowing faculty. Prayer should be direct and specific, and should always be accompanied by a positive receptivity. God cannot answer prayers which have no meaning. The answer to prayer is in the prayer when it is uttered or thought. We do not pray aright when we are in opposition to the fundamental harmony. The whole teaching of Jesus, relative to prayer, is that God will answer when we pray aright. Jesus points to the fact if we, being human and consequently limited, know how to give good gifts to our children, how much more will God give good things to those who ask and he explicitly tells us to ask directly for what we want. If we ask for bread we shall not receive a stone. This *must* be true if we are dealing with intelligence.

"Therefore all things whatsoever ye would that men should do to you, do ye even so to them: for this is the law and the prophets." How clearly this states the Law while referring to the prophets who had already taught the same law.

THE BROTHERHOOD OF MAN

If this brotherhood of man were recognized and practiced by the world at large, all war, poverty, and need would vanish from the face of the earth. They are creations of the finite mind and were never intended to be. God views all as a perfect whole; our divisions are only apparent, they can never be real. Hate generates hate, love begets love, and peace brings its own reward. Again let us not fall under the illusion that we can possibly measure life from the short range experience of that period of time between the cradle and the grave. Life is everlasting and we are eternal beings. Eventually love overcometh and exalteth itself above all, for love is a synonym for the Eternal Heart of the universe.

GOD AND CREATION

We are to know the truth by its fruits. The sure estimate of reality is ever evidenced by its worth in actual living. We are not to separate life from living nor God from His creation. One is the Cause, the other is the effect. The invisible things of God are manifested through the visible, and unless the invisible thought and desire of man is in line with Truth his acts will fall into error. While we are told not to judge we are clearly warned not to fall under the illusion of accepting the false for the true.

ENTERING THE KINGDOM OF REALITY

It is not everyone who says, "Lord, Lord," who enters the kingdom of harmony; only those who do the will of love can enter. The temple of Truth is approached by the pure in heart and entered by those who serve but one master which is the Truth.

In no way can this passage be misconstrued to mean or even to suggest anything like the theological hell. Jesus never taught the popular concept of hell. He was laying down a philosophy of life for time, as well as for eternity. He knew that eternity must be made up of different times. To suppose an eternity without the element of time, is to suppose an impossibility for it means to suppose an unexpressed existence.

The wise man builds his house on the solid rock of Truth and not on the shifting sands of unstability. He measures causes by effects and estimates reality by that which is real and enduring. The foolish man, living only in sense perception, has no measure for reality and builds his home on false opinion and erroneous concept; the vicissitudes of fortune upset his frail building, the storms of experience tear the walls apart, while the edifice falls about him in ruins. Truth alone endures to Eternal Day.

. .
.

And Jesus said unto the centurion,
Go thy way; and as thou hast believed, so be it done unto thee.
And his servant was healed in the self-same hour.

MATTHEW 8

. .
.

THE HEALING OF THE CENTURION'S SERVANT

In Matthew 8 we have a beautiful story in the life of Jesus, which shows his great compassion and love for humanity. The healing of the centurion's servant. Note that the centurion would not allow Jesus to come to his house but asked him to speak the word only.

The centurion, being a man in authority on the physical plane, recognized that Jesus exercised like authority on the mental and spiritual planes. Without this recognition he would not have known that Jesus could heal his servant by the power of his word. "Speak the word only, and my servant shall be healed." It is no wonder that Jesus marveled at this faith. And how quickly was this faith answered by an affirmative response from a heart of love and a mind of understanding. "Go thy way; and as thou hast believed, so be it done unto thee."

How simple the words, yet how fraught with meaning! What majesty and what might! From whence came the power of this spoken word? Is it not necessary to suppose that the word of man, when spoken in compliance with the law of Truth, is also all-powerful? We cannot believe that Jesus had an occult power not possessed by other men. To think this would be superstition. We certainly cannot suppose that he was especially endowed with power from on high, for this would be to believe in a partial God. There is but one logical answer to the power of Jesus. He believed what he taught and so completely lived his teachings that he was able to demonstrate them. But we should remember that his will was ever in accord with the Divine Mind.

. .
.

And, behold, they brought to him a man sick of the palsy, lying on a bed: and Jesus, seeing their faith, said unto the sick of the palsy,

Son, be of good cheer; thy sins be forgiven thee.

And, behold, certain of the scribes said within themselves, This man blasphemeth.

And Jesus, knowing their thoughts, said, Wherefore think ye evil in your hearts? For whether is easier, to say, Thy sins be forgiven thee; or to say, Arise, and walk?

But that ye may know that the Son of man hath power on earth to forgive sins, (then saith he to the sick of the palsy,)

Arise, take up thy bed, and go unto thine house.

No man putteth a piece of new cloth unto an old garment; for that which is put in to fill it up taketh from the garment, and the rent is made worse.

Neither do men put new wine into old bottles; else the bottles break, and the wine runneth out, and the bottles perish: but they put new wine into new bottles, and both are preserved.

And, behold, a woman, which was diseased with an issue of blood twelve years, came behind him, and touched the hem of his garment:

For she said within herself, If I may but touch his garment, I shall be whole,

But Jesus turned him about; and when he saw her, he said, Daughter, be of good comfort; thy faith hath made thee whole.

And the woman was made whole from that hour.

And when Jesus departed thence, two blind men followed him, crying, and saying, Thou Son of David, have mercy on us.

And when he was come into the house, the blind men came
to him: and Jesus saith unto them,

Believe ye that I am able to do this? They said unto him, Yea,
Lord.

Then touched he their eyes, saying, According to your faith
be it unto you.

MATTHEW 9

. .
.

JESUS FORGIVES A MAN
AND HEALS HIM

Now some of the scribes who heard Jesus tell the sick man that his
sins were forgiven said he blasphemed God in attempting to forgive sins. But Jesus, reading their thoughts and knowing what was
in their minds, asked them if it were easier to forgive or to heal? In
order to prove his position he healed the man.

This incident has to do with a great psychological law. If one
labors under a great burden of past mistakes he devitalizes his body
and if the condemnation is great enough it might render the body
incapable of moving. Jesus, seeing that the sick man was laboring
under a load of condemnation, told him that his sins were forgiven.
This removed the weight from the man's consciousness, making it
possible for him to receive the healing word.

Would Jesus have forgiven the man if he thought that God held
anything against him? Certainly not. He knew that the Eternal
Heart is one of love and that God forgives from the foundation of
the universe. Indeed he knew that the Divine Mind is too pure to
behold evil and knows nothing about sin.

GOD KNOWS NO EVIL

If God knew sin He would be a sinner, for what the Infinite Mind knows must BE. Sin or mistakes are outside the province of Reality; Jesus knew this. He also knew that while man labors under the sense of condemnation the burden of his thought weighs him to the dust. Being able to read thought he knew just what step to take in relieving the burden of this man's mind before telling him to arise and walk.

We shall do well to remember this lesson. How often we condemn when we should forgive, how often censure when we might praise. What untold grief of heart might be relieved by words of cheer and forgiveness. Especially should this lesson be remembered in the training of children, for they so readily respond to the thought of others.

Remembering that the Spirit holds no evil toward any and that God is Love, we should emulate this divine lesson and forgive all, that our hearts may be free from the burden of our own condemnation.

NEW CLOTH AND OLD GARMENTS

In saying that "no man puts a piece of new cloth on an old garment or new wine into old bottles," Jesus was teaching a lesson in religious development. We are continuously living a new life and when the old and the new do not fit nicely together, the old, being no longer able to contain the new, should be discarded. Every day we must expect new revelations of old truths. We should never lose sight of the fact that the soul is on the pathway of an endless and ever-expanding experience and that only by expansion can it evolve. This does not mean that we should cast away any good which the old has to offer, but that we convert it into a greater good. Accepting the lessons and experiences of the past and taking the best from everything, we should press boldly forward, looking ever for the Truth and ever ascending higher and higher into the heavens of reality.

There is no limit to the possibility inherent in all men. Let the timid soul put its complete trust in good and press bravely on.

* *
*

And, behold, a woman, which was diseased . . . came behind
  him, and touched the hem of his garment:
For she said within herself, If I may but touch his garment, I
  shall be whole.

MATTHEW 9

* *
*

"THY FAITH HATH MADE THEE WHOLE"

It is said that Jesus was aware of the diseased woman's presence and turned to her with the words, "Thy faith hath made thee whole." This is a lesson in impersonal healing, showing that the spiritually minded are surrounded by an atmosphere of wholeness, the very presence of which has a power of healing. Again, we find Jesus saying, "Thy faith hath made thee whole." This is in line with his whole teaching, that it is done unto men as they believe. "And the woman was made whole from that hour."

In healing the blind men Jesus asked if they believed he was able to restore their vision, and upon their acceptance of his ability to do so, he said, "According to your faith be it unto you." Again he was showing the necessity of faith and belief as supreme requisites in the demonstrating of spiritual power.

It is well to remember that back of our eyesight stands the eternal vision, the ultimate spiritual perception, the all-seeing eye; could we completely realize this, its corresponding effect would open our eyes and we would see.

. .
.

Heal the sick, cleanse the lepers, raise the dead, cast out devils: freely ye have received, freely give.

Provide neither gold, nor silver, nor brass in your purses, Nor scrip for your journey, neither two coats, neither shoes, nor yet staves; for the workman is worthy of his meat.

And into whatsoever city or town ye shall enter, enquire who in it is worthy; and there abide till ye go thence.

And when ye come into an house, salute it. And if the house be worthy, let your peace come upon it: but if it be not worthy, let your peace return to you.

But beware of men; for they will deliver you up to the councils, and they will scourge you in their synagogues:

And ye shall be brought before governors and kings for my sake, for a testimony against them and the Gentiles.

But when they deliver you up, take no thought how or what ye shall speak: for it shall be given you in that same hour what ye shall speak.

For it is not ye that speak, but the Spirit of your Father which speaketh in you. . . . there is nothing covered, that shall not be revealed; and hid, that shall not be known.

Are not two sparrows sold for a farthing? and one of them
shall not fall on the ground without your Father.

But the very hairs of your head are all numbered. Fear ye not
therefore, ye are of more value than many sparrows.

And a man's foes shall be they of his own household.

He that findeth his life shall lose it: and he that loseth his life
for my sake shall find it.

He that receiveth you, receiveth me; and he that receiveth
me, receiveth him that sent me.

He that receiveth a prophet in the name of a prophet shall receive a prophet's reward; and he that receiveth a righteous man in the name of a righteous man shall receive a
righteous man's reward.

And whosoever shall give to drink unto one of these little
ones a cup of cold water only in the name of a disciple,
verily, I say unto you, he shall in no wise lose his reward.

MATTHEW 10

THE LAW OF CIRCULATION

"Freely ye have received, freely give." When the law of circulation
is retarded, stagnation sets in. It is only as we allow the Divine current to flow through us and on and out that we really express life.
The law of giving and receiving is definite. Emerson tells us to beware of holding too much good in our hands.

Because of the unity underlying all life, no man lives entirely
unto himself, but through himself he lives unto the whole, which
whole embodies all other lives. Therefore, "He that findeth his life
shall lose it: and he that loseth his life shall find it."

When a man's thought rests entirely upon himself he becomes abnormal and unhappy; but when he gives himself with enthusiasm to any legitimate purpose, losing himself in the thing which he is doing, he becomes normal and happy. Only as much life enters into us as we can conceive, and we conceive of life in the larger sense, only when there is complete abandonment to it.

The losing of personality in the great sea of life which surrounds us makes possible the flow of this life through our own livingness, producing the inevitable reaction of a greater livingness in our own lives. Let the one who is sad, depressed, or unhappy find some altruistic purpose into which he may pour his whole being and he will find a new inflow of life of which he has never dreamed.

WHOM SHALL WE TRY TO HELP

But Jesus was wise in the ways of the world as well as in heavenly wisdom, and he counseled his followers against attempting to help people when they wished no help; he said, "And when ye come into an house, salute it. And if the house be worthy, let your peace come upon it: but if it be not worthy, let your peace return to you." This is a lesson which sincere students of the truth often discover to their great chagrin. People do not always receive their message and when this happens there should be no controversy, no argument, and no sense of disturbance, but, abiding in a conviction of the ultimate acceptance of truth by all, they should let their peace return unto themselves and go calmly on their way, unprejudiced, noncombative, but certain of themselves. If, however, they are called upon to defend their faith they should remember that the spirit indwelling their lives will put the very words into their mouths which they should speak; for the great teacher said, "It is not ye that speak but the spirit of your Father which speaketh in you." Never forget that there is an indwelling Spirit which *knows*.

NOTHING CAN BE HIDDEN

In saying, "There is nothing covered, that shall not be revealed; and hid, that shall not be known," Jesus was referring to that law of cause and effect which is immutable. To the mind which knows all there are no secrets and from the all-seeing eye nothing is hidden. When we seek to cover things we are but attempting to put a lid over an energy which will not be suppressed. The Cosmic ear hears everything, the Eternal Mind knows all things, and the law of cause and effect brings everything to pass in its time. A normal life is one which has nothing to conceal, but which is lived with spontaneous open-mindedness and complete receptivity to the Good.

A MAN'S FOES

"And a man's foes shall be they of his own household." There are no enemies external to our own mind. This is one of the most difficult problems to understand and simple as it sounds it penetrates the depths of creative causation. Nothing can happen to us unless it happens through us. That which we refuse to accept, to us, cannot be, and that, which to us *is,* cannot help becoming a reality. But someone will say, "I did not conceive of this evil which came upon me; it was not in my mind." The question then arises, can any particular evil be real to one if he refuses to entertain it in his thought? The answer must forever be, *it cannot*. This is one of those "hard sayings" which is difficult to understand, but the principle involved is plain.

If we can divorce our lives from the thought of evil, from receptivity to it, if we can bring our mentality to a place where it no longer conceives evil, then evil cannot exist for us. The proof of this doctrine remains for individual conviction, through experience, but it is well worth trying.

THE REWARD OF TRUE VISIONING

"He that receiveth a prophet in the name of a prophet shall receive a prophet's reward: and he that receiveth a righteous man in the name of a righteous man shall receive a righteous man's reward." There comes to each, the logical and exact result of his own receptivity. To each, life brings the reward of his own visioning; to the pure all is pure, to the righteous all is righteous, and to the good all is good. The reward of merit is an objective outcome of merit itself and not a thing superimposed by any Divine Mandate. Each man is rewarded not *by* virtue but *through* virtue.

An interesting experiment along this line would be for one to penetrate the mistakes of human frailty, under whatever guise, and demand of himself that he see the reality hidden behind the veil of illusion. To speak to his fellow man as though he were addressing a god; to overlook the lie and see the truth, to behold a perfect image, hidden in the form of clay. Who knows what such visioning might bring forth? The lame would walk, the blind would see, the untruthful would desert his lies, and we would find ourselves in the company of angelic presences, peopling our world with forms of beauty and thoughts of peace, bringing heaven to earth and revealing the God incarnated in everything.

. .
.

The blind receive their sight, and the lame walk, the lepers are cleansed, and the deaf hear, the dead are raised up, and the poor have the Gospel preached to them.

And as they departed, Jesus began to say unto the multitude concerning John, What went ye out into the wilderness to see? A reed shaken with the wind?

But what went ye out for to see? A man clothed in soft raiment? Behold, they that wear soft clothing are in kings' houses.

But what went ye out for to see? A prophet? yea, I say unto you, and more than a prophet. For this is he, of whom it is written, Behold, I send my messenger before thy face, which shall prepare thy way before thee.

Verily I say unto you, Among them that are born of women there hath not risen a greater than John the Baptist; notwithstanding he that is least in the kingdom of heaven is greater than he.

But whereunto shall I liken this generation? It is like unto children sitting in the markets, and calling unto their fellows, and saying, We have piped unto you, and ye have not danced; we have mourned unto you, and ye have not lamented.

For John came neither eating nor drinking, and they say, He hath a devil.

The Son of man came eating and drinking, and they say, Behold a man gluttonous, and a wine-bibber, a friend of publicans and sinners. But Wisdom is justified of her children.

At that time Jesus answered and said, I thank thee, O Father, Lord of heaven and earth, because thou hast hid these things from the wise and prudent, and hast revealed them unto babes.

Even so, Father; for so it seemed good in thy sight.

All things are delivered unto me of my Father: and no man knoweth the Son, but the Father; neither knoweth any man the Father, save the Son, and he to whomsoever the Son will reveal him.

Come unto me, all ye that labour and are heavy laden, and I will give you rest.

Take my yoke upon you, and learn of me; for I am meek and lowly in heart: and ye shall find rest unto your souls.

MATTHEW 11

· ·
·

"WISDOM IS JUSTIFIED OF HER CHILDREN"

"Wisdom is justified of her children." Jesus had been questioning his hearers about John the Baptist. "For John came neither eating nor drinking, and they say, He hath a devil. The Son of man came eating and drinking, and they say, Behold a man gluttonous, and a wine-bibber, a friend of publicans and sinners." But, "Wisdom is justified of her children."

This shows that the world ever finds some flaw in human character. If a man fasts he is possessed of peculiar ideas and if he feasts he is a materialist and a glutton. But Jesus would have us understand that virtue consists neither in eating nor drinking nor yet in abstaining from eating and drinking. "Wisdom is justified of her children." A man may desire to fast and be wise, or he may desire to feast and still be wise. Virtue is independent of any material form which it may take. The children of wisdom look to the inner and not to the outer for justification. Wisdom knows neither publican nor sinner but is conscious only of herself though she may dress in many garments.

If one believes that virtue consists in fasting, then virtue appears to him through fasting, but to him who finds no virtue in fasting, feasting may appear to be a greater virtue. We are overconcerned with nonessentials, straining at gnats while swallowing mountains of superstition.

THE CHILDLIKE FAITH

Jesus teaches that a childlike mind is more receptive to Truth than an overintellectual person, who must have too rational an explanation to those truths which cannot be intellectualized, but which must be accepted on their face value. For instance, who could explain why he lives? The self-evident fact of living is the only explanation possible or necessary. In the whole life and through the entire teaching of this marvelous man we find a childlike faith in the universe and an implicit trust in the goodness of God. Judging his work by its results and its influence on succeeding ages we are compelled to accept the fact that "Wisdom is justified of her children."

THE REAL FATHER AND SON

"And no man knoweth the Son, but the Father; neither knoweth any man the Father, save the Son, and he to whomsoever the Son will reveal him."

What reasonable explanation can we find to this passage unless we look for some hidden meaning behind these words of the great teacher? God alone knows the real son, forever hidden in the bosom of the Father. To God this idea of sonship must be pure, complete, and perfect; divine, holy, and indestructible. With our present limited vision we neither see nor know the *real* son but the Father within knows and understands. "Neither knoweth any man the Father, save the Son, and he to whomsoever the Son will reveal him." God is revealed through the Son and the Son reveals himself to other sons when he realizes that God is his life. This implies a direct relationship between God and man.

If one would know God he must penetrate deeply into his own nature for here alone can he find Him. If he would reveal God to his fellow men he must do so by living such a Godlike life that the Divine Essence flows through him to others. The only way to know God is to be like Him, and while this may seem discouraging in our present stage of evolution we should remember that we have but started on an eternal ladder which ever spirals upward.

When Jesus said to come unto him and find rest, did he mean that we should or could come unto his personality? Of course not. Jesus knew that his human personality would soon be dissolved in his divine individuality. He knew that he was soon to leave this world and go on to a deeper realization of life, truth, and beauty.

It is evident, then, that he was referring to his understanding of life when he told all who are weary to come unto him and find rest.

Had he not already explained that God indwells every soul? He was inviting people to penetrate more deeply into their own natures if they would find peace and comfort. This has ever been the lesson taught by the illumined and this has been the reason for their illumination.

Here is the lesson; we can find God only within ourselves and God can work for us only by working through us. God reveals Himself directly through the Son. The Son reveals God when he realizes that God is already within him. This understanding would not produce an undue conceit nor would it set man in the temple of God *as* God; but it would place a true estimate of value on the life of man.

THE POWER AT THE
HEART OF GOD

Peace is the power at the heart of God. It is through the revelation of the self to the self that one understands life, that he approaches the power which is at the heart of God. This comes through a recognition of the unity of the individual with the Spirit back of, in, and through all.

The problem of philosophy is to unite the Infinite with the finite, to join the abstract with the concrete, to find a meeting place between the Absolute and the relative, to unify with First Cause. The same problem confronts religion and is indeed, its whole purpose, to unify man with God. This is also true of science but from a different angle; science seeks to join causes with effects and by so doing to make practical use of its knowledge. Science is really spiritual while philosophy leads to true religion. Science is the handmaid of religion and philosophy.

THE GREAT SEARCH

The world seeks a solution of its great riddle—the apparent separation between God and man, between life and what it does, between the invisible and the visible, between the Father and the Son, and until this riddle is solved there can be no peace.

Peace is an inner calm, stable and certain, obtained through man's knowledge of what he believes and why. Without knowledge there is no lasting peace. Nothing can bring peace but the revelation of the individual to himself and a recognition of his direct relationship to the universe. He must know that he is an eternal being on the pathway of life, with certainty behind him, certainty before him, and certainty accompanying him all the way.

Peace is brought about through a conscious unity of the personal man with the inner principle of his life, that underlying current, flowing from a divine center, pressing ever outward into expression. But this can never come by proxy. We can hire others to work for us, to care for our physical needs, but no one can live for us. This we must do for ourselves.

THE NEED OF SPIRITUAL
EXPERIENCE

We need spiritual experience, a firsthand knowledge of life and reality. There is no medium between God and man, nothing between life and living, between heaven and hell but an idea. But an idea has no real value until it becomes an experience.

In conversation we assume great knowledge of religion and philosophy but how much do we really experience? We can know only that which we experience. All great religions have taught truth but it means nothing to us unless it becomes our truth.

We need spiritual experience. We shall never know peace until we embody it; we shall never know Truth until we become Truth; and we cannot know God unless we sense Him within our own being. The Spirit is ever giving, but we must take. What life does for us must be done through us.

It is useless for a troubled mind to beseech God to bring peace to it. *God Is Peace,* and we can approach this wonderful presence only as we turn from all that is opposed to it. It is useless to ask God to save sinners from eternal damnation since the Divine Mind conceived neither hell nor devil. If the Deity could know these things they would have a real existence. God knows only peace, and peace is the power at the heart of the Eternal Mind. Back of all is eternal goodness, loving-kindness, and everlasting blessedness.

Spiritual experience is deep, calm, and self-assertive; it is the result of actually realizing that presence which binds all together in one complete Whole. This experience comes in the stillness of the soul when the outer voice is quiet, when the tempest of mortal strife is abated; it is a quickening of the inner man to an eternal reality.

Spiritual experience is not an opinion, it is a fact. Spirituality may be defined as the atmosphere of good, the realization of God. It cannot, and does not, borrow its light from another, no matter how great or noble he may be; it springs from within, coming from that never-failing fountain of life, which quenches every thirst, whose source is in eternity; the wellspring of self-existence. It is a revelation of the self to the self, putting one back on the track of his own self-dependence on Spirit, his own at-one-ment with reality.

THE CAUSE OF
HUMAN TROUBLES

I believe all human troubles, sickness, sin, accident, poverty, and calamity to be the result of ignorance of the true relationship between man and the Spirit. The integrity of the universe cannot be questioned nor doubted. The Spirit *must be,* and is, *perfect.* That which is back of everything must be good, must be complete, must be love and harmony. When we are out of harmony with some special good it is because we are off the track along that particular line of the activity of Spirit.

But how are we to regain the lost Paradise? Only through soul culture and by careful self-analysis. What is my viewpoint of life? This is a question each should ask himself. What do I feel my relationship to the great Whole to be? What do I believe about the Cause back of all? From whence come discouragement, fear, doubt, and calamity? They cannot proceed from the eternal. Source, that perfect fount of life, the inexhaustible One. Therefore they must come from my own deluded consciousness. They cannot be born of the Truth. The Truth is God and God is free, happy, peaceful, and ever poised in His own Being. I must set myself right with the universe. I must find the way back to the central fire if I am to be warmed. I must find the source if I am to be supplied. I must be like God if I wish to realize His Spirit in my own life.

A change of consciousness does not come by simply willing or wishing. It is not easy to hold the mental attention to an ideal while the human experience is discordant, but—it is possible. Knowing the truth is not a process of self-hypnotism but one of a gradual unfoldment of the inner self.

We do not say peace when there is no peace; if there is none we should strive to find the reason for its apparent absence. The reason is always written in the confusion of human thought.

WORLD PEACE

World Peace will appear when the nations, realizing that there is good enough to go around, learn to live together in harmony. This is a matter of self-training among the different peoples, an international understanding. This international consciousness is being born to the nations today and will yet shine full-orbed. Then we shall cease to have wars.

The world is made up of individual members so we must begin with the unit. We cannot carry discord into harmony for discord is a lack of the proper appreciation of harmony. As a straight line finds no abiding place in a curve, so discord finds no abiding place in harmony. We cannot carry our troubles to the Spirit for the Spirit is untroubled. We approach God only through His own nature.

If one wishes to experience peace he must first become peaceful in his own thought. Careful self-training will do this; watching one's thought and carefully discarding such mental attitudes as are of a destructive nature; this is possible for all. The Divine ear cannot listen to discord. Become peaceful and you will find peace.

HOW TO APPROACH THE SPIRIT

If we wish to come to the Spirit for the healing of our wounds let us come in peace and with spontaneous joy, for the Spirit is joy; let us come with thanksgiving also, for a thankful heart is in harmony with life. But we must come in quiet confidence, with an open and receptive mind, and a believing heart; naturally, sanely, expectantly. In this way we are entering the portals of reality, clad in garments of righteousness.

We often think what we require is money, friends and physical healing. After these things do those who are outside a knowledge of the law seek; and they do well, for we need all these things, but they are the effects of right relationships to life. All people need some form of healing. Most people are unhappy, few have any realization of permanent peace. We seek fragments when the whole is at hand. How illogical to think that anything can rise higher than its source. The universe is a perfect, undivided whole and healing can take place only when one is unified with it. How can anyone, then, be healed in part? Let us seek wholeness above all else.

If we would come to the universal wholeness, we must approach it through the law of its own nature. This means that we must give our undivided attention to the spiritual unit back of all things. Since all else is included within this unit, we find our particular good only through unity with life. This conscious unity makes our mind receptive to completion, since life itself is complete. This perception is always an inner light, for the individual can use only such knowledge as he inwardly possesses. In reality we know God or Truth only as we ourselves embody God or Truth. And since it is impossible to embody anything outside of oneself, this knowledge must be an inner light. The Truth itself is infinite but we do not embody the Infinite, except in degree. To the degree that we do embody reality we become poised and powerful.

THE PURPOSE OF RELIGIOUS SCIENCE

The whole purpose of Religious Science is to reconcile the apparent separation of the spiritual world, which must be perfect, with the material world, which appears imperfect. The spiritual world is the cause of the material; we are spiritual beings governed by mental law. Only that world can appear to us which we mentally perceive. Man's experience is the logical outcome of his inner vision; his horizon is limited to the confines of his own consciousness. Wherever this consciousness lacks a true perception its outward expression will lack proper harmony. This is why we are taught to be transformed by the renewing of our minds. Peace comes as our own thought becomes tranquil; it is never conceived through confusion, for confusion begets confusion, and is analogous to the blind man leading the blind, the result of which is that both fall into the ditch. Those who take up the sword shall perish by it.

We should approach confusion with peace until the mentality is brought to a point of nonrecognition of it; it will then cease to be. This statement can be vouched for only by those who have proven it. Since no one lives by proxy, but each unto himself, every individual must make the test in his own soul.

. .
.

And Jesus knew their thoughts, and said unto them, Every
kingdom divided against itself is brought to desolation;

and every city or house divided against itself shall not
stand;

Either make the tree good, and his fruit good; or else make
the tree corrupt, and his fruit corrupt: for the tree is
known by his fruit.

O generation of vipers, how can ye, being evil, speak good
things? for out of the abundance of the heart the mouth
speaketh.

A good man, out of the good treasure of the heart, bringeth
forth good things:

And an evil man, out of the evil treasure bringeth forth evil
things.

But I say unto you, that every idle word that man shall speak,
they shall give account thereof in the day of judgment.

For by thy words thou shalt be justified, and by thy words
thou shalt be condemned. . . .

But he answered and said unto him that told him, Who is my
mother? and who are my brethren?

Whosoever shall do the will of my Father which is in heaven,
the same is my brother, and sister, and mother.

MATTHEW 12

"AND JESUS KNEW THEIR THOUGHTS"

"And Jesus knew their thoughts." Jesus was consciously psychic,
that is, he had an extended vision which enabled him to read the
thoughts of others without going into a trance. To be able to dis-

cern the thoughts of others, without entering an abnormal state, is a development which will ultimately come to all. But in our present state of evolution this would not always be a pleasant experience, and *will not be* until we have learned to think constructively. But according to the narrative, Jesus "knew their thoughts." He had been healing a man possessed of unclean thoughts and the priests had reasoned within themselves that his power to do this was of the "evil one."

Jesus, perceiving their mental process, told them that a house divided against itself cannot stand and that if he cast out evil by the power of evil, then evil would be a power divided against itself. But, he said, "if I cast out devils by the Spirit of God, then the kingdom of God is come unto you."

Here is the lesson. We cannot do good by continuing to do evil nor can we heal evil except by the power of good. To all sincere students of Spiritual Science this lesson is a guide post, pointing to the fact that the thought of good must ever overcome and completely put to rout any thought of evil or any thought that is less than good. By the presence of good, evil is cast out, just as by the presence of light the darkness disappears.

GOOD THOUGHTS AND A GOOD HARVEST

A good tree produces good fruit, so good thoughts bear a harvest of good deeds, while evil consumes itself in the flame of its own fire. If a man's life produces good deeds the man is himself good: and this, no matter what his particular religious belief may or may not be.

The mouth speaks from the heart. It is impossible for a man to conceal himself. In every act, word, or gesture he stands revealed as he is, and not as he would have himself appear to be. From the universe nothing is or can be hidden; the very walls have ears and the mirror of life cannot help reflecting back to us that which we really are.

Jesus plainly tells us that we are held accountable for the very words which we speak. No man ever lived who placed a greater power in the word. By our words we are justified or condemned. The word may be considered to be the complete thought and act of man. There must be a thought before there can be an act and a thinker before there can be any thought. The thinker condemns or justifies himself through his thought.

We should think that only, which we wish to have happen, and wish only for that which is good. If our thought divides itself between good and evil, then our experiences will be mixed; part good and part evil. When we learn to think from the standpoint of good alone, we will overcome evil and all that harms us will disappear from our lives.

THE FATHER–MOTHER GOD

It is related that while Jesus was talking he was told that his mother and brethren waited to speak with him. "But he answering said unto him that told him, Who is my mother? and who are my brethren?" He then told them that whoever does the will of God is his mother, sister, and brother. We are not to suppose by this that he did not care for his earthly parents or friends. He was explaining that anyone who lives in harmony with the Truth, automatically becomes the brother or the mother of all.

This is a lesson in the brotherhood of man. God is the Androgynous Principle, the Father and Mother of all. Our earthly parents symbolize this heavenly parentage. Jesus was a consciously cosmic soul who recognized his unity with all. He knew that love must become universal before it can reach its maturity. Hence he said that all who live in harmony with the Truth are brothers in it.

* *
*

Whosoever hath, to him shall be given, and he shall have more abundance; but whosoever hath not, from him shall be taken away even that he hath.

For this people's heart is waxed gross, and their ears are dull of hearing, and their eyes they have closed; lest at any time they should see with their eyes, and hear with their ears, and should understand with their heart, and should be converted, and I should heal them.

But blessed are your eyes, for they see; and your ears, for they hear.

For verily I say unto you, That many prophets and righteous men have desired to see those things which ye see, and have not seen them; and to hear those things which ye hear, and have not heard them.

Another parable put he forth unto them, saying, The kingdom of heaven is like to a grain of mustard seed, which a man took, and sowed in his field:

Which indeed is the least of all seeds; but when it is grown it is the greatest among herbs, and becometh a tree, so that the birds of the air come and lodge in the branches thereof.

Another parable spake he unto them; The kingdom of heaven is like unto leaven, which a woman took and hid in three measures of meal, till the whole was leavened.

The kingdom of heaven is like unto treasure hid in a field; the which when a man hath found, he hideth, and for joy thereof goeth and selleth all that he hath, and buyeth that field.

The kingdom of heaven is like unto a merchantman seeking goodly pearls: Who, when he had found one pearl of great price, went and sold all that he had, and bought it.

MATTHEW 13

TO HIM WHO HATH SHALL BE GIVEN

"Whosoever hath, to him shall be given, and he shall have more abundance; but whosoever hath not, from him shall be taken away even that he hath."

This certainly sounds like a very hard saying and is most discouraging to one who has not fathomed the depths of its meaning. We appear to have little enough, and to have this little withdrawn from our small possessions seems more than we can bear. And for us to feel that those who already have are to receive more, sounds unfair.

Let us examine this saying in the light of an understanding of the law of cause and effect. We know that everything works from within out, that subtle causes lie hidden in the creative power of the mind. The mind is the builder and sustainer, the creator, and distributor, and unless the mind conceives of itself as possessing good things it will not appear to possess them. From the objective world of such an one, even that which he has will be taken away. This is but another way of stating the law of cause and effect, that immutable principle which governs all things.

THE CONCEPT OF
A SUCCESSFUL MAN

Could we see the mentality of a successful man, we should find the imprint of success written in bold letters across the doorway of his consciousness. The successful man is sure of himself, sure of what he is doing, certain of the outcome of his undertakings. As much gathers more, as like attracts like, so success breeds greater success and conviction is attended by certainty. The whole teaching of Jesus is to have faith and to believe. He placed a greater value on faith and belief than anyone who has ever taught spiritual truth. We are to believe in ourselves because we have first penetrated the invisible cause back of the real self. We are to have absolute faith in our work because we have positive conviction of the inner power which enables us to do the work.

But to those who believe only in failure the law comes in corresponding measure, measuring back to them the logical outcome of their beliefs. The habitual failure bears across the threshold of his thought an image of his inability to attain. The old law says that what little he has shall be withdrawn until he has learned the lesson of life and action.

Each should train himself, and do so consciously, to conceive of himself as a success. Sailing on that immense sea of livingness, upon whose bosom we are all carried forward, we should go from success to greater success. All thoughts of failure or depression must be erased from the mentality, and positive thoughts of achievement should take their place. Have faith in God, in life, and in your fellow man. Know that right is might. Get some degree of real conviction and stay with it. The Cosmic Mind is neither wishy-washy nor willy-nilly. It is positive, certain of itself and sure of the outcome.

THE SEEING EYE

"But blessed are your eyes, for they see; and your ears, for they hear." What is it that the eye should see and the ear hear? Do not all people's eyes see and their ears hear? No. But few, indeed, looking, see, or listening, hear.

We are to see that Spirit creates all things by the power of Its own word and that we are spiritual beings. We are to hear that inner voice of Truth which is ever proclaiming the freedom of all life, the eternal unity of God with man. It is useless for those who have never experienced this inner seeing and hearing to deny its reality. A man might as well say there is no meadow because he has never seen one. The world needs spiritual experience as it needs bread and butter. Men need spiritual convictions as they need meat and drink. And with spiritual conviction comes all else. To those who have shall be given.

THE KINGDOM AND THE MUSTARD SEED

"The kingdom of heaven is like a grain of mustard seed." From a knowledge of mental action we know that a constructive idea, planted or buried in the subjective field of mind, tends to grow into a real condition. Jesus could not have chosen a more comprehensive way to illustrate his point.

THE KINGDOM IS LIKE LEAVEN

"The kingdom of heaven is like leaven." We know that thoughts planted in mind have the power to chemicalize opposing ideas and leaven the whole lump of subjectivity. In this way ideas gradually permeate the mind and influence all thought and action. If the idea is of heaven it will certainly bring about a heavenly state.

THE PEARL OF GREAT PRICE

The kingdom of heaven is likened unto a pearl of great price for which a man will sell all that he has, that he may possess it. This, perhaps, best explains the way of the illumined. To them, the kingdom of heaven has meant everything, and has been above all else. We find them going away by themselves that they may more completely enjoy this inner realization of their relationship to the Whole. A divine companionship has ever attended such on the pathway of human experience. The description of the things they have seen, felt, and heard, constitutes some of the most valuable lessons the world has ever learned.

The only news we have of heaven has come through the consciousness of men and to those few who have penetrated the veil of illusion and entered the realms of deeper reality, we owe a debt that cannot be paid in any other terms than those of appreciation and thanksgiving.

That the illumined have had experiences which the average man cannot conceive of is certain, and that anyone who wills to know Truth may know it, is evident to all who make the attempt. But let us not forget that spiritual experiences are normal, natural, and rational. The illumined have always had rational intellects and well-balanced mentalities.

No experience is salutary unless it be gained while in a normal state of mind. Too great a warning cannot be given against any attempt to break through the veil when in any other but a perfectly normal mental state.

Jesus lived in the spiritual world just as normally as we live in the material and just as consciously. And what is the spiritual world? And where is it? It is right here could we but see it. Behind everything material, stands the spiritual, supporting it, and without which there could be no material.

. .
.

And he called the multitude, and said unto them, Hear, and
    understand: not that which goeth into the mouth defileth
    a man; but that which cometh out of the mouth, this de-
    fileth a man.
Every plant, which my heavenly Father hath not planted,
    shall be rooted up.

If the blind lead the blind, both shall fall into the ditch.

Then Jesus answered and said unto her, O woman, great is thy faith: be it unto thee even as thou wilt. And her daughter was made whole from that very hour.

MATTHEW 15

. .
.

THAT WHICH DEFILES

Not what we eat or drink, but what we think defiles. The issues of life are from within. If a man is clean in his mind, then is he clean indeed. We must keep the mental house free from any thought which contradicts the truth of being.

Life is what consciousness makes it. This is a great realization. Experience may appear to disclaim this fact, but the principle involved is an immutable one and cannot be shaken any more than the integrity of the universe can be violated.

Let each resolve to be true to himself, true to his inner light, true to the Truth as he understands it. When every man learns to speak the truth a complete salvation will come to the world. If one thinks impurity, then his acts will be impure. If his thought dwells on purity and Truth then his acts, reflecting his mind, will make him pure and true.

Every plant which is not of God's planting shall be rooted up. In the long run all that does not belong to the heavenly kingdom will be destroyed. Truth alone can endure. All wickedness, sin, and mistake will eventually be done away with and righteousness will be enshrined in every heart.

WHEN THE BLIND LEAD THE BLIND

"If the blind lead the blind, both shall fall into the ditch." We must be careful what kind of thought we are following. We must test all ideas to see whether they are of the Truth. It is a mistake to accept every man's philosophy simply because it sounds plausible. We are to be on guard against accepting that which is not true. And let us remember this, the Truth is simple, direct, and always self-evident.

False ideas heaped upon other false ideas make bad matters worse. The whole confusion of the world arises from fundamental errors of thought. Chief among these errors, and the father to a greater part of the others, is a belief in duality. The belief in duality supposes that evil is equal to good, that a suppositional devil divides the kingdom of Truth with good. Such things cannot be. Remember the teaching of Moses, that "God is One." If, on the other hand, we accept that evil has a power equal to good, then we must fall into the ditch of our own confusion.

To believe in the good alone may seem fallacious to many but he who believes thus will find his path lighted by a torch which flickers not, nor fails.

. .
.

Then said Jesus unto his disciples, If any man will come after me, let him deny himself, and take up his cross and follow me.

For whosoever will save his life shall lose it: and whosoever will lose his life for my sake shall find it.

MATTHEW 16

. .
.

WHO WOULD SAVE HIS LIFE
SHALL LOSE IT

This is another of those mystical sayings of Jesus which must be carefully considered before accepting it. Does God demand that we give up everything if we are to enter the kingdom of heaven? Of course not! God is the All-Being, as well as the All-Knowing: and the All-Being cannot wish or will that anyone should be less than It is. To suppose that God wills us to be limited is to contradict the Divine Nature. God's only will is to Be, and for all to Be, for God can conceive of man only as part of Himself.

It must be, then, that what we are to lose is the sense of the possibility of living apart from Life. We find ourselves in the Divine Idea, immersed in the Infinite Godhead, one with the Perfect Whole. But should we think that we, of ourselves, without this relationship rightly established, can be, or can express, then we cut the cord that binds us to the main power line and lose what little power we have.

We are powerful only as we unite with Power. We are weak when we desert this Power. Not because God is jealous, but because this is the way things work. The idea of a false renunciation, of the giving up of all pleasure and benefits in this life, is not even suggested in the teachings of Jesus. Self-effacement, the neglect of the body, starving and abusing the physical instrument, the belief that we must be unhappy and poor in order to serve the Truth, all these are immature ideas which deny the divine birthright of the soul, the incarnated spirit of the Most High within us.

When we are willing to lose a personal sense of responsibility, when we let go of the thought of isolation and claim a real unity with God, then we lose the personal and find the universal. But remember, as the greater always includes the lesser, so the Universal always includes the personal, which is a personification of Itself.

Man is to lose the small estimate of himself, the isolated person, and is to find the greater reality, the incarnated and real ego. The image of the Father cannot be defaced nor can all the wit or the sham of man really obliterate this image. The Eternal Light is God and this light illumines the pathway of the personal when there are no obstructions.

Who leans on the Truth, throwing all, with an undivided attention, on the scales of reality will find them balancing rightly, through the great law of compensation, which weighs and measures everything exactly as it is.

• •
•

And when they were come to the multitude, there came to
    him a certain man, kneeling down to him, and saying,
Lord, have mercy on my son: for he is lunatic, and sore
    vexed: for offtimes he falleth into the fire, and oft into the
    water. And I brought him to thy disciples, and they could
    not cure him.
Then Jesus answered and said, O faithless and perverse gen-
    eration, how long shall I be with you! how long shall I suf-
    fer you! Bring him hither to me.
And Jesus rebuked the devil; and he departed out of him: and
    the child was cured from that very hour.
Then came the disciples to Jesus apart, and said, Why could
    not we cast him out?
And Jesus said unto them, Because of your unbelief: for ver-
    ily I say unto you, If ye have faith as a grain of mustard
    seed, ye shall say unto this mountain, Remove hence to
    yonder place; and it shall remove;

And nothing shall be impossible unto you. Howbeit this kind goeth not out but by prayer and fasting.

MATTHEW 17

. .
.

FASTING AND PRAYER

In the healing of the lunatic, when his disciples had failed, Jesus showed that the more real the apparent separation from good, the more certain we should be that with God all things are possible.

Some ideas are gotten rid of only through fasting and prayer. But we are not to suppose that the physical act of fasting or the metaphysical act of prayer can move the throne of grace to a kindness which is otherwise withheld. God plays no favorites and the law of the universe cannot reverse its own nature. Fasting and prayer often do bring our thought closer to Reality, not because of the fasting or the prayer, but because they open up greater fields of receptivity in our minds.

If one wishes to embody an ideal and is willing to give up all else to attain it, then is he fasting and praying. He is sublimating an old idea with a new and better one. If he is willing to abstain from the old and cling to the new, then he is giving greater reality to the new and in this way contacting the law from a more affirmative angle.

A steadfast determination to attain some purpose, the letting go of all that opposes it, a complete reliance upon the Law of Good and an unqualified trust in Spirit, this is the true fasting and real prayer.

The scientist, in profound thought and meditation, before his problem, deserting all to solve it, is praying a true prayer to the principle of his science. The poet, waiting in the silence of his own soul for inspiration, is praying that he may invoke the spirit of poetry to his listening ear. The sculptor, chiseling at his marble, withholding food from his mouth, contemplating on the beauty to be brought forth from naught, prays to his god of art, and the farmer, kneeling beside his cabbage patch, trusts in the natural Law of Good to bring his seed to harvest.

We live in a fasting and praying world but often do not read the signs aright. We are too used to the outward sign to realize its inward significance. The world is much better than it knows or feels itself to be.

HEALING THE LUNATIC

What majesty and might do we see in the calm words of Jesus! "Bring him hither to me." No doubt is here, no sense of approaching failure, no lack of trust in the perfect law which governs all. "And Jesus rebuked the devil; and he departed out of him."

Surely this lesson should teach us that evil is but an obsession and, from the standpoint of eternal Reality, a complete illusion. Could we cast out evil from our thought if evil were a real entity or had actual power? The answer is self-evident, we could not. Evil flees before Reality and to the mind which knows it, evil is not.

.˙.

Verily I say unto you, Except ye be converted, and become
as little children, ye shall not enter into the kingdom of
heaven.

Whosoever therefore shall humble himself as this little child,
the same is greatest in the kingdom of heaven.

And whoso shall receive one such little child in my name receiveth me.

Verily I say unto you, Whatsoever ye shall bind on earth shall
be bound in heaven; and whatsoever ye shall loose on
earth shall be loosed in heaven.

Again I say unto you, That if two of you shall agree on earth
as touching any thing that they shall ask, it shall be done
for them of my Father which is in heaven.

For where two or three are gathered together in my name,
there am I in the midst of them.

Then came Peter to him, and said, Lord, how oft shall
my brother sin against me, and I forgive him? till seven
times?

Jesus saith unto him, I say not unto thee, Until seven times;
but, until seventy times seven.

MATTHEW 18

• •
•

AS LITTLE CHILDREN

We must become as little children. How we long for a return of
that simple trust in life which children have; in their minds there
are no doubts, they have not yet learned that they are sinners, des-
titute of divine guidance and spiritual life. The life of the child is
lived in natural goodness. God is natural goodness. The prison
walls of false experience soon build themselves into barriers, shut-

ting out the light and the child grows into a man, often losing his sense of that inner guide leading his footsteps aright.

We must return the way we came. As little children, who know that life is good and to be trusted, we are to approach our problems as though they were not; approaching them in this manner, they will vanish.

Let not the materialist deny us this right, nor the unbelieving cast any reflection of his blindness before our eyes. There is a wisdom and power not of the flesh which springs perennially from the inner life—all powerful and all wise.

"WHATSOEVER YE SHALL BIND ON EARTH"

Next we come to a passage difficult to understand and one which has caused confusion in many minds. "Whatsoever ye shall bind on earth shall be bound in heaven; and whatsoever ye shall loose on earth shall be loosed in heaven."

A superficial reading of this passage might lead one to suppose that this old earth is the last chance of the soul. But this is not the meaning of the text. It means simply this, the experience of death cannot change all. As a man has lived while on earth so he will continue to live after death. If he has been pure he will continue to be pure. If he has been otherwise he will continue to be otherwise.

False experience will continue until the lesson is learned, until the soul turns from that which hurts to its greater good. The spirit of man is of like nature to the spirit of God and it is impossible for the spirit of God to remain in darkness. The next life is a logical continuation of this one and could not be otherwise.

DIVINE FORGIVENESS

In the next passage Jesus clearly explains the meaning of divine for-giveness. He says that we should forgive until seventy times seven. This is but another way of saying that forgiveness is eternal and ever available. What a load is dropped from the shoulders of per-sonal responsibility when we realize that the Eternal Mind holds naught against anyone. But to those who feel this is unfair it will be a hard saying. "What!" says one, "are not my virtues to be rewarded above those who have none?" O, foolish one and blind, what do you know about virtue? Has your life always been beyond reproach? Have you never fallen short of the divine calling? Who are you to point the finger of scorn at your brother? The man who feels self-righteousness rise from his petty virtues lives a life of self-delusion.

Know this. Virtue does not know that it is virtuous and could it know it, it would immediately become vicious. Virtue is sweet, like the morning dew, soft as the evening star, and brilliant as the noon-day sun. Could the dew tell why it is sweet, the star say why its light is soft, or the sun say why it shines?

When we learn to put away our petty virtues with our petty vices then shall we see clearly, not what either virtue or vice is, but what Truth is.

The mind which condemns understands not the truth of being, and the heart which would shut the door of its bosom to the one who is mistaken, strangles its own life, closing its eyes to a greater vision. The biggest life is the one which includes the most.

Not that we foster vice or place a premium upon wrong doing, but that we understand the frailties of human nature and learn to overlook much. To him who loves much, much is forgiven.

. .
.

But Jesus said,

> Suffer little children, and forbid them not, to come unto
> me; for of such is the kingdom of heaven.

And he said unto him,

> Why callest thou me good? there is none good but one,
> that is, God:

But if thou wilt enter into life, keep the commandments.

MATTHEW 19

• •
•

"There is none good but one, that is, God": This reminds us of
the teaching of Moses that "God is One." We are to realize that
goodness shines through all people and all things and that it is always the goodness of God.

The moment we feel any goodness or life apart from the One,
that moment we isolate ourselves and soon become exhausted.
God is the natural Goodness running through all alike, and we are
to see this God in all if we are to see aright. We are powerful, good,
and complete only as we are unified with Reality which is God, the
Father of all.

• •
•

Jesus answered and said unto them,

> Verily I say unto you, If ye have faith, and doubt not, ye
> shall not only do this which is done to the fig tree,

But also if ye shall say unto this mountain, Be thou removed,
> and be thou cast into the sea; it shall be done.

And all things, whatsoever ye shall ask in prayer, believing,
> ye shall receive.

MATTHEW 21

• •
•

A FORMULA
FOR EFFECTIVE PRAYER

Here is a formula for true and effective prayer. The things we need we are to ask for and we are to believe that we receive them. This plumbs the very depths of the metaphysical and psychological law of our being and explains the possibility of an answer to our prayers.

When we pray we are to believe that we have. We are surrounded by a universal law which is creative. It moves from the thought to the thing. Unless there is first an image it cannot move, for there would be nothing for it to move toward. Prayer, which is a mental act, must accept its own answer as an image in mind, before the divine energies can play upon it and make it productive.

As we must plant a seed before we can reap a harvest, so we must believe before our prayers can be answered. Prayer should reach a point of acceptance, an unqualified and undisputed place of agreement. Let us take the mental image of our desires to the bosom of the creative life and here make them known by impressing them upon it with positive belief. If we do this our prayers will be answered.

But let us remember that true prayer is always universal. There can be no good to us alone, but only as that good is for all. This does not mean that we are to refrain from asking what we wish for but that we should wish only for that which is good. For instance, it is good to have a home; it is good for all people to have homes while here on earth; it is right to ask for one, but it would not be right to ask for one belonging to another.

If we wish to pray for a home we should take the idea of a house with us into the silence and meditate upon its actual being. We should believe that we have and own a home, but we should leave the idea free to fulfill itself without any definite choosing of how, where, or why. In this way we pray aright and when we so pray, we pray effectively.

God wills us to have everything. As we express life we fulfill God's law of abundance but we do this only as we realize that there is good enough to go around.

. .

But as touching the resurrection of the dead, have ye not
    read that which was spoken unto you by God, saying,
I am the God of Abraham, and the God of Isaac, and the God
    of Jacob?
God is not the God of the dead, but of the living.
Jesus said unto him, Thou shalt love the Lord thy God with
    all thy heart, and with all thy soul, and with all thy mind.
This is the first and great commandment. And the second is
    like unto it,
Thou shalt love thy neighbour as thyself.
On these two commandments hang all the Law and the
    Prophets.

MATTHEW 22

THE RESURRECTION OF THE DEAD

In his teaching on immortality, Jesus was explaining that God knows nothing about death. If the principle of that which lives is Life, then it cannot know death. To suppose that Life knows death is to deny the Principle of Life.

"God is not the God of the dead, but of the living." Which means that all live unto him. The experience of death is but the laying off of an old garment and the donning of a new one. The resurrection body is already formed within us and will be carried along when we pass from this plane.

The experience of death, or change, is necessary, else we would become so enamored of this life that we would not be willing to go on to another. When the body is no longer a fit instrument through which the soul may function it is laid aside and a new one used. God sees only the expression, never the process through which the expression takes place. Hence God knows no decay or death.

THE TWO GREAT COMMANDMENTS

The two great commandments are to love God and our brother man. On these hang all the law and the prophets. Love is a complete unity with life and we cannot enter this state unless we are in unity with all that lives, for all life is One. To love God alone is not enough for this would exclude our fellow man. To love our fellow man alone is not sufficient, for this would be too limited a concept of God.

When we realize that God and man are One and not two, we shall love both. We shall love man, as an expression of God, and God, as the Life Principle in all.

From this teaching we are not to suppose that we are to love that in each other which does not savor of right. We are to love the right alone. We are to look for God in each other and love this God, forgetting all else. But would this compel us to accept from people that which is not good? Of course not! It is not necessary for one to make a door mat of himself in proving that God is love, for this would be like suffering for righteousness' sake, which is always a mistake.

We should be wise in the ways of the world as well as imbued with Divine wisdom. We are not to mistake a counterfeit for the real, nor accept every man's doctrine lest we disagree. The Truth is positive but noncombative; it is sure of itself but never argumentative. It deserts dishonesty and receives honesty; loves sincerity and abhors deceit. Above all else, the Truth is wise. It represents the all-seeing eye from which nothing can be hidden.

The student of Truth will receive all that comes in the name of the Lord, that is, all that is of the Truth; all else will fall by its own weight.

.·.

Watch and pray that ye enter not into temptation: the spirit
    indeed is willing, but the flesh is weak. . . .
Then said Jesus unto him,
Put up again thy sword into his place: for all they that take up
    the sword shall perish with the sword.

MATTHEW 26

.·.

HISTORY PROVES THE
REALITY OF TRUTH

As we glance over the pages of history this saying of Jesus stands sure and true. Those nations who have risen by the sword have fallen among the ruins of their own false hopes. History has proven that strife begets strife and the way of the transgressor is hard.

In international strife all nations are beaten, in so far as they have taken up the sword in hate, avarice, or lust. We do not recognize that apparent power which lasts for a day, for it is but a false gesture defeating its own purpose as falseness ever must.

Jesus, speaking from the viewpoint of Eternal Truth, said that all who take up the sword shall perish by it. We should remember that life is not well reasoned unless we reason from the standpoint of the Eternal Soul. Those who have given the best to the world have always been best remembered by it, and most loved throughout the ages. If we attempt to measure existence from this short span of life it would not be explained and we would find no real answer to life itself.

Hate begets hate and strife produces strife. Love alone overcomes all and justifies the eternity of her dominion.

. .
.

A certain man had two sons; and the younger of them said to
his father, Father, give me the portion of goods that falleth to me. And he divided unto them his living.
And not many days after, the younger son gathered all together, and took his journey into a far country, and there
wasted his substance with riotous living.
And when he had spent all, there arose a mighty famine in
that land; and he began to be in want.
And he went and joined himself to a citizen of that country;
and he sent him into his fields to feed swine.
And he would fain have filled his belly with the husks that the
swine did eat: and no man gave unto him.

And when he came to himself, he said, How many hired servants of my father's have bread enough, and to spare, and I perish with hunger!

I will arise and go to my father, and will say unto him, Father, I have sinned against Heaven, and before thee, and am no more worthy to be called thy son: make me as one of thy hired servants.

And he arose, and came to his father. But when he was yet a great way off, his father saw him, and had compassion, and ran, and fell on his neck, and kissed him.

And the son said unto him, Father, I have sinned against Heaven, and in thy sight, and am no more worthy to be called thy son.

But the father said to his servants, Bring forth the best robe, and put it on him; and put a ring on his hand, and shoes on his feet:

And bring hither the fatted calf, and kill it; and let us eat, and be merry: for this my son was dead, and is alive again; he was lost, and is found.

And they began to be merry.

Now his elder son was in the field: and as he came and drew nigh to the house, he heard music and dancing.

And he called one of the servants, and asked what these things meant.

And he said unto him, Thy brother is come; and thy father hath killed the fatted calf, because he hath received him safe and sound.

And he was angry, and would not go in: therefore came his father out, and entreated him.

And he answering said to his father, Lo, these many many years do I serve thee, neither transgressed I at any time thy commandment; and yet thou never gavest me a kid, that I might make merry with my friends:

But as soon as this thy son was come, which hath devoured thy living with harlots, thou hast killed for him the fatted calf.

And he said unto him, Son, thou art ever with me, and all that I have is thine.

It was meet that we should make merry and be glad: for this thy brother was dead, and is alive again; and was lost, and is found.

LUKE 15

GOD TURNS TO US
AS WE TURN TO HIM

The parable of the Prodigal Son constitutes one of the greatest spiritual lessons in the history of religious education. It is an attempt, on the part of the Great Teacher, to show that God turns to us as we turn to Him; that there is a reciprocal action between the Universal and the individual mind; that the Spirit is ready to help us whenever we turn to It.

The greatest lesson we have to learn is the unity of Love and Law; the necessity of law in shaping a divine individuality and the necessity of experience in awakening to this divine individuality.

God is Love and God is Law; the *love* of God is omnipresent and the *law* of God is omnipresent. The love of God is the Divine givingness, the eternal outpouring of Spirit through Its creation. The law of God is the law of cause and effect which says that we can have only what we take: since this taking is a mental and spiritual as well as a physical act, we can take only that to which we are receptive. Jesus taught, it is done unto us as we really believe. "The thought is ever father to the act."

INDIVIDUALITY AND CHOICE

Our individuality enables us to choose, but ignorance of the true nature of being often causes us to choose evil rather than good. The question might be asked, "Why are we able to choose evil?" The answer is that we would not be individualities unless we could exercise the power of self-choice. Experience alone will teach us what is for our best good, until finally we shall all desire the good. This is the meaning of heaven or harmony.

All are subject to the reign of law; consequently, all are subject, under the law, to the logical outcome of choice. Evil is not a thing of itself, but is the wrong use of the law. If we believe only in evil this is all we can experience; if, on the other hand, we believe only in the Law of Good—we shall experience good. This immutable law governs all things and binds all together in one logical sequence.

The universe is a perfect unit; it is not divided, neither is it divisible. It is governed by law which is cold, relentless, unfeeling, mathematical, exact, and certain. We are the offspring of love, but subject to law.

THE TWO SONS

In presenting the parable of the Prodigal Son to his listeners, Jesus began by saying that the Father, which is the Universal Spirit, had two sons, meaning that, as the son of God, man has the right of self-choice. This carries with it the possibility of an apparent duality (but, of course, not a real one), and the possibility of experiencing good and evil. Moses referred to the same thing when he said that he had set a blessing and a curse before the Children of Israel, that they must *choose* whom they would serve. The two sons, referred to in this story, allegorically denote the two states of consciousness necessary to real individuality. Man is a conscious, self-knowing mind, equipped with volition and choice; he is an individual and can do as he chooses.

GOD DOES NOT ARGUE

"A certain man had two sons: And the younger of them said to his father: Father, give me the portion of goods that falleth to me. And he divided unto them his living." When the younger son asked for his portion of goods God did not argue with him. God never argues. To argue is to suppose an opposite and God has no opposite. We argue to arrive at a correct conclusion; God is already the correct conclusion of all things, therefore, He does not need to argue. Plotinus tells us that nature never argues, that it contemplates itself, that its contemplation creates a form through which it may become expressed. Undoubtedly this is the whole meaning and process of creation.

"And he divided unto them his living." There was no argument. God did not tell the son that it would be far better for him to remain at home. He did not say that he might come to want and suffer, perhaps starve. He did not tell him anything: "He divided unto them his living." The Universe gives us what we ask; experience alone will teach us what is best to have. "He divided unto them his living." No clearer statement of individuality could possibly be inferred than this. The son received exactly what he asked for, no more and certainly no less. The cup of his acceptance was filled from the universal horn of plenty; he could do with it as he chose.

THE FAR COUNTRY

"And not many days after, the younger son gathered all together, and took his journey into a far country, and there wasted his substance with riotous living." When the son had received his share of goods he went into a "far country." We are all in this "far country," for it symbolizes the descent of the soul, or the outer rim of spiritual existence. It does not mean a place, but rather a state of consciousness. If God is Omnipresent, we cannot escape the Divine Presence, so this "far country" means a state of consciousness which has separated itself from the eternal good. The true meaning, I believe, of the "far country" would be a conscious separation from God, an isolated state, one in which there appears to be no remembrance of God as an actual, living, and ever-present reality; one where man feels himself to be separated and entirely apart from the Eternal Good.

This "far country" has as real a meaning today as it did in the hills of Galilee, nearly two thousand years ago, for all have come from heaven and nearly all feel the isolation of this seeming apartness from the Eternal Good. Indeed, the whole endeavor of mankind is to return to the Father's House.

WHY WE ARE IN WANT

"And there wasted his substance with riotous living. And when he had spent all, there arose a mighty famine in that land; and he began to be in want." When one separates himself from the Divine Fire he becomes an isolated spark. We are strong only when united with Life. As soon as our consciousness is detached from spiritual wholeness we can no longer draw from that inexhaustible reservoir of eternal existence, so we become exhausted—there is nothing to fall back upon.

Life is one perfect Wholeness. The universe is a Unit. God is One. It is impossible for man to feel separated from the Spirit without feeling lost and in want. This is why Jesus said that he could do nothing of Himself, but could work only as the currents of divinity ran through his personal mentality. That subtle something which runs through all things and which we call *"the thing Itself,"* that *energy* without which nothing can be energized, that *life* without which nothing can live, that *power* without which nothing can move and that *Spirit* without which nothing can be—IS GOD. It is only as we live in conscious union with the Spirit, and consciously let It work through us that we really live.

THE FALLEN MAN

So the prodigal son "began to be in want. And he went and joined himself to a citizen of that country; and he sent him into the fields to feed swine." The symbolism here is most interesting for it perfectly depicts the state of humanity while in the "far country." The "citizen" referred to, means the attempt, on the part of man, to find some cause outside of Spirit. Man seeks to league himself with material forces alone, not realizing there can be nothing outside the Unit. Most of us seek the cause in the effect and unknowingly put the cart before the horse, not realizing that the flower is already in the seed, that effects must follow causes. There can be no true alliance apart from life and no good apart from a unity with the Whole. "And he sent him into his fields to feed swine." Jesus was a Jew. The Jews did not consider the meat of the swine lawful to eat; consequently he used this term in order to show how completely the prodigal son had fallen from his high estate; he must even be compelled to feed the despised swine. This demonstrated that his state of being was so low that it would be impossible for it to be any worse. It had reached the outer rim of reality and was flat on its back. We are reminded here of another symbol, one used in the Old Testament, that of the serpent, which cast Adam and Eve out of the Garden of Eden. The serpent meant the outer rim of spiritual existence; the Life Principle viewed from an isolated and materialistic basis. The worship of material existence, apart from God, cast Adam and Eve from the Garden of Perfection. The attempt to live in effects, apart from the true cause, always does this. But, lest we should become discouraged, we remember that Moses lifted up the serpent in the wilderness and that those who looked upon it were healed.

The serpent means the Life Principle. Viewed from a material basis alone, it casts us from a perfect state; lifted up, that is— viewed from a true meaning of the Unity of God, it heals. Here is the choice again, only stated in different words. The difference is not in the thing itself, but in the way we look at it.

NO ONE GIVES TO US
BUT OURSELVES

"And he fain would have filled his belly with the husks that the swine did eat: and no man gave unto him." How true this is; no one can give unto us but ourselves and no one can rob us but ourselves. "There are no gods to say us nay, for we are the life we live." In our greatest extremity, in the moment of great need and dire distress, who can help or serve us? All of our troubles come from an isolated sense of being; *we alone* can return to the "Father's House."

The question might be asked, "Where was God and why did He not come to the rescue of His beloved son? Did He not care—was He heedless about His son's welfare? Why did God allow such a thing to happen?" There is only one answer to all questions of this nature; God is always God, and man can always do as he pleases. He would not be an individual unless this were possible. The Father is never conscious of incompletion. The Father's House is always open, the latch string ever hanging out; the door always ajar, but man must enter if he wishes to abide within.

Harmony can never become discord. The truth can never pro- duce a lie. God can never be less than God. Could God enter into a field of strife then He would not be God. God cannot enter the pig pen. We cannot contract the Infinite but we can expand the finite. "And no man gave unto him." It is always thus.

THE GREAT AWAKENING

"And when he came to himself, he said, How many hired servants of my father's have bread enough, and to spare, and I perish with hunger!" "And when he came to himself." This is the great awakening, the moment in which we now live; in this moment we are asking this question of ourselves! Is there not plenty in the universe? Why do we want? In this divine awakening there seems to be an inner witness who remembers that we came from a heavenly state. There seems to be an answer from that great within which says the Father's House is filled with peace, power, and plenty. The universe is not limited. It is abundance. It is lavish. It is extravagant, nothing can be taken from, nor added to it. Creation is the play of life upon itself.

We know, by intuition, that there is something beyond what we have so far consciously experienced in this world. Poets have sung of it and there are moments, in the life of all, when the veil seems thin between and we almost enter into the heavenly state. This is the meaning of coming to one's self. We are still in the awakening state. We have not yet consciously entered the state of perfect wholeness. We know that it is a reality, and that we shall yet attain this reality. Nothing can dislodge this inner and intuitive perception from our mentality; we know it as certainly as we know that we live. This is God in us knowing Himself. We are awakening to the realization that the universe is perfect. It is complete. It gives. It is love. It is good and wills only good to all alike.

SELF–CONDEMNATION

"The prodigal said, I will arise and go to my father, and will say unto him, Father, I have sinned against Heaven and in thy sight; I am no more worthy to be called thy son: make me as one of thy hired servants." This represents a theological state of mind which is quite common to all of us; one of self-condemnation and personal distrust; it is morbid and detrimental to our welfare; a theological state of introspective morbidity which might be classed as one of our worst mental diseases. Self-condemnation is always destructive and should never be indulged in by anyone, it is always a mistake. There is no question but all of us have done that which is not for the best; from this viewpoint all have been sinners, because all have fallen short of the Divine Calling. If we have sinned, it is because we have been ignorant of our true nature and because experience was necessary to bring us to ourselves.

AND THE FATHER SAW
HIM AFAR OFF

"And he arose, and came to his father. But when he was yet a great way off, his father saw him and had compassion, and ran, and fell on his neck, and kissed him." This is the most perfect lesson ever taught by the Great Teacher. "When he was yet a great way off, his father saw him and ran, and fell on his neck, and kissed him." This means that God turns to us as we turn to Him. A more beautiful thought could not be given than this! There is always a reciprocal action between the Universal and the individual mind. As we look at God, God looks at us. Is it not true that when we look at God, God is looking through us, at Himself?

God comes to us as we come to Him. "It is done unto us as we believe." "Act as though I am and I will be."

GOD DOES NOT CONDEMN

And the son said unto him, Father, I have sinned against Heaven, and in thy sight, and am no more worthy to be called thy son.

But the father said to his servants, Bring forth quickly the best robe, and put it on him; and put a ring on his hand, and shoes on his feet.

And bring hither the fatted calf, and kill it; and let us eat and be merry, for this my son was dead, and is alive again; he was lost and is found. And they began to be merry.

The great lesson to learn here is that God never reproaches us and never condemns.

He took my book, all stained and blotted,
And gave me a new one all unspotted,
And into my sad eyes smiled,
Do better now, my child.

God did not say to the returning son, "You miserable sinner, you are no more worthy to be called my son." He did not say, "I will see what I can do about saving your lost soul. I will spill the blood of my most precious son in hopes that by this atonement your life may be made eternal." He did not say, "You are a worm of the dust and I will grind you under my feet in order that you may know that I am God and the supreme power of the universe." No, God did not say any of these atrocious things. What the Father did say was, "Bring forth quickly the best robe, and put it on him: and put a ring on his hand and shoes on his feet." Here Jesus is showing that God is Love and knows nothing about hate.

GOD KNOWS NO SIN

Perhaps the most significant thing in this paragraph is the fact that God did not answer his son when he talked about being a sinner. The Father talked about something else. This is one of the most wonderful lessons in the whole story. God does not know evil and therefore cannot talk about, or conceive it in any form. If God could know evil then evil would be an eternal reality. God is sinless and perfect and nothing can reflect itself in the Divine, save a perfect image. If God could know sin He would be a sinner. It is enough to know that this cannot be.

THE BEST ROBE

Now the "best robe" was a seamless garment and typifies a state of complete unity, as does the ring. The robe is seamless and the ring is without beginning or end. It begins everywhere and ends nowhere.

It is like eternity and eternal reality. It perfectly describes the Divine Nature. "The fatted calf" represents the abundance of God's love and providence.

THE FATHER'S HOUSE ALWAYS OPEN

And so the son found everything in the Father's House just as he had left it. Nothing had changed and he was made welcome to all the divine stores. But he had to return to find joy and peace forevermore. How wonderful is Reality! While we may have seemed to be away from it, it has ever remained the same and is ever ready to reveal itself to us. All we have to do is to go halfway; that is, turn to it and it will turn to us. The Truth known is instantly demonstrated; for the Truth is Changeless Reality and cannot come and go. No matter how long we may have been away from Reality in our thought, it is always here, ready to spring forth, full-orbed, into expression. No matter how long a room may have been darkened the entrance of light instantly illuminates it. What becomes of the darkness when the light enters? Where did it come from and where does it go?

It is difficult to comprehend such an infinite possibility as an instantaneous reconciliation with the universe; we demonstrate this only in degrees, because our consciousness is not yet fitted to perceive the wholeness of complete perfection.

THE STAY-AT-HOME SON

Now the elder son was in the field: and as he came and drew
nigh to the house, he heard music and dancing.

And he called unto him, one of the servants and inquired
what these things might be and he said, Thy brother is
come; and thy father hath killed the fatted calf, because
he hath received him safe and sound.

And he was angry and would not go in; therefore came his
father out, and entreated him.

And he answering said to his father, Lo, these many years do I
serve thee,—and yet thou never gavest me a kid that I
might make merry with my friends.

And he said unto him, Son, thou art ever with me, and all
that I have is thine.

How human the stay-at-home son was and what a theological attitude he took in regard to his younger brother. He had not entered
himself and was not willing that anyone else should enter. His real attitude was that God should damn everything that he, himself, did not
like or believe. He was puffed up with self-righteousness and personal conceit, filled with petty vanity, and fuming with anger over his
brother's welcome home. I expect that we meet him in ourselves
nearly every day, in our personal experiences with other people, in
our intolerant attitude and uncharitableness toward others who do
not think as we think.

But God knows as little about self-rightcousness as He knows
about evil, for both are false; therefore, He said unto the elder son,
"Thou art ever with me, and all that I have is thine." This implies
that the elder son had missed the mark as well as the younger, for

he had been living in the midst of plenty and had not recognized it. He needed but to have asked and he would have received all that the father had. Both sons were foolish but it is a question which was the more completely deluded.

THE APPLICATION
OF THE STORY

But to bring this story down to our own experience; for it is a lesson for everyone and for all time. We live in the midst of eternal good, but it can only be to us what we believe it to be. We are at the mouth of the river, we must let down our own buckets if we wish them to be filled with the pure waters of Reality.

We are surrounded by a spirit of living intelligence and eternal givingness, love, goodness, and power that wishes to express itself through us. There is a divine urge within ever pushing us forward toward the goal. We also are surrounded by an immutable law of cause and effect, because of our divine individuality and the necessity of experience in order to come to a realization of what, and who we are, we are subject to the causes which we have set in motion. All is love, and yet all is law. Both love and law are perfect and we, as individuals, can experience only what we really believe and act upon.

GOD CAN ONLY GIVE US
WHAT WE TAKE

God cannot give us anything, unless we are in a mental condition to receive the gift. The law cannot do anything for us unless it does it through us. Belief is absolutely necessary to right demonstration.

We are on the path of experience, just waking to the real fact of our true being; as we awake we find that we are surrounded by many false conditions, but there is something within, which remembers the real state. If one will sit in quiet contemplation of good, as an inner-presence, he will experience the good which he contemplates. He can do this only as he turns from that which is evil and dwells on the good alone. The universe will not be divided.

THE UNIVERSE HOLDS
NOTHING AGAINST US

The universe holds nothing against us. No matter how many mistakes we have made we are still perfect beings within, and the within may become the without, if we will carefully train ourselves to listen to the inner voice of truth which speaks to all people in their moments of quietness and solitude.

There is nothing in the universe that wishes evil to anyone; indeed, it is only as we experience good that God is expressed through us. The more completely we realize good, happiness, and success, the more perfectly do we express God and the more of God do we become; that is, the more does God become personified through us.

As the prodigal returned to his father's house, so must *we* return, not with a morbid mind, but consciously and definitely, with a direct intent of mind and a complete concentration of purpose. The journey back should be fraught with happiness and joyful expectation. We shall be met with a smile from the universe and shall be folded in the arms of love forever.

THE ETERNAL COMPLETION

Substance and supply exist eternally in the Father's House; health, happiness, and success are native to the divine land of our heavenly home, and God Himself shall be our Host. More we could not ask, more could not be given than that which has been given from the foundations of the universe.

Discord, misery, and unhappiness are the result of a misuse of our true nature, the result of ignorance. Ignorance of the law excuses no one from its effects; but knowledge clothes us in the seamless robe, while wisdom puts the ring of completion on our finger and understanding feeds us with the fat of the land.

No one who has tried this has failed; it would be impossible to do so. If any have thought they have failed let them realize that somewhere, *they* have fallen short of the divine calling. The Truth cannot fail for it is God, the Absolute and Unconditioned One, who is the Truth.

Let us no longer fight the old; let us no longer remember that we were once on the outer rim; let us forget the past and live in the eternal present of God's happy smile. Today is good; tomorrow will be even better and that vista of tomorrows that stretches down the bright eternities of an endless future will all be good, for the nature of reality cannot change.

. .

Verily, verily, I say unto thee, Except a man be born again, he cannot see the kingdom of God.

Verily, verily, I say unto thee, Except a man be born of water and of the Spirit, he cannot enter into the kingdom of God.

That which is born of the flesh is flesh; and that which is born of the Spirit is spirit.

Marvel not that I said unto thee, Ye must be born again.

The wind bloweth where it listeth, and thou hearest the sound thereof, but canst not tell whence it cometh and whither it goeth: so is every one that is born of the Spirit.

Verily, verily, I say unto thee, We speak that we do know, and testify that we have seen: and ye receive not our witness.

If I have told you earthly things, and ye believe not, how shall ye believe, if I tell you of heavenly things?

And no man hath ascended up to heaven, but he that came down from heaven, even the Son of man which is in heaven.

JOHN 3

. .

THE NEW BIRTH

"Except a man be born again, he cannot see the kingdom of God." Jesus is referring to the heavenly birth which means being born into the knowledge of Truth. He refers to this as being born of water and Spirit.

The symbol of water is used to express the idea of a complete immersion in Spirit. As water flows in and around, so we are immersed in an everlasting Spirit which flows around, in and through us. To be immersed in water symbolizes our recognition that we are surrounded by pure Spirit. It is the outward sign of an inner conviction. But water alone cannot make us completely clean or whole. We must be born of the Spirit, for, "that which is born of the Spirit is Spirit."

Man partakes of the Divine Nature and the Divine Nature is man. The recognition of this is being born of the Spirit. But we cannot be born of the Spirit unless we do the will of the Spirit and the will of the Spirit is goodness, peace, mercy, justice, and truth. It is conscious union with God.

The new birth comes not by observation nor by loud proclamation, but through an inner sense of reality. We cannot tell where this comes from if we look to outward things, as it proceeds from the innermost parts of our own being.

HEAVEN

"And no man hath ascended up to heaven, but he that came down from heaven, even the Son of man which is in heaven." Here is another of those hidden meanings which place Jesus among the great mystics. He says that no man can go to heaven unless he came from heaven and that he can neither go to, nor come from heaven unless he is already there.

This is in line with the idea that the Truth knows neither yesterday, today, nor tomorrow. It knows sequence but not time. Only that can return to heaven which was born in heaven, and since heaven is not a place, but a state of consciousness, the return must be a recognition that heaven is already within. The son of man, who is also the son of God, is already in heaven and knows it not.

THE SON OF MAN

As Moses lifted up the serpent in the wilderness, so Jesus tells us must the son of man also be lifted up. By looking on and believing in this son we are saved. Jesus could not have been referring to his own personality, for he knew that this would soon be taken from the sight of humanity. We must look for a deeper meaning.

We must be lifted up, that is, we must realize our divine nature and relationship to the Truth of God. This relationship is one of complete unity. The cross represents the tree of life and may also be thought of as the tree of unity.

When Moses lifted the serpent those who looked upon it were healed. This means that as they understood the Life Principle to be spiritual and not material they were healed. This understanding produced a consciousness of unity which had healing power. The Life Principle is either looked upon as material or spiritual. When looked upon as material it casts us from the garden of Eden—the garden of the soul. The Life Principle viewed only as *matter* is death, but viewed as *life* and *unity* it becomes life everlasting. Moses elevated the Life Principle and Jesus did the same. The son of man must be lifted up even as Moses lifted up the Life Principle, symbolized by the serpent.

The son of man is every man who ever lived or ever will live. Our life is from spirit and not from matter. This viewpoint is the truth and truth alone makes us free. We come into everlasting life as we elevate this inner principle to a sense of the unity of man with God. Each must lift himself up to the cross of the Tree of Life, thus unifying himself with reality. The concept is glorious and the reward certain. The revelation of the self to the self. This is the great lesson of lessons.

. .
.

Whosoever drinketh of the water that I shall give him shall
    never thirst,
But the water that I shall give him shall be in him a well of
    water springing up into everlasting life.
The hour cometh, and now is, when the true worshipers
    shall worship the Father in spirit and in truth: for the Father seeketh such to worship him.
God is a Spirit: and they that worship him must worship him
    in spirit and in truth.

JOHN 4

. .
.

THE WOMAN AT THE WELL

In his conversation with the woman of Samaria Jesus again revealed his psychic powers, for he told the woman her exact condition. So impressed was she with this power that she asked her friends to come and see a man who had told her all about herself.

Notice that Jesus did not condemn the woman. He taught her; he told her that God is Universal Spirit, an ever-present reality and the eternal urge in all life.

To Jesus this Spirit was an indwelling, as well as an overdwelling Presence, a conscious Intelligence to which one may come for help and guidance.

· ·
·

Verily, verily, I say unto you, The Son can do nothing of himself, but what he seeth the Father do:

For what things soever he doeth, these also doeth the Son likewise.

For the Father loveth the Son, and sheweth him all things that himself doeth:

And he will shew him greater works than these, that ye may marvel.

For as the Father raiseth up the dead, and quickeneth them, even so the Son quickeneth whom he will.

Verily, verily, I say unto you, He that heareth my word, and believeth on him that sent me,

Hath everlasting life, and shall not come into condemnation; but is passed from death unto life.

For as the Father hath life in himself, so hath he given to the Son to have life in himself;

I can of mine own self do nothing: as I hear, I judge: and my judgment is just;

Because I seek not mine own will, but the will of the Father which hath sent me.

JOHN 5

· ·
·

WHEN WE ARE STRONG

"The son can do nothing of himself." We are strong only as we are in unity with good, which is God. But the Father showeth the son, that is, it is revealed to us, through the innermost parts of our being, that there is a complete unity, a perfect wholeness. As this concept of unity takes place it brings with it great authority. The Father quickens the son, the son quickens whom he will.

Here is a lesson in practical Religious Science. As the subjective state of thought becomes unified with goodness and love, it automatically reflects these in whatsoever direction the thought goes. The tendency of this inner thought sets the tendency of the outward life.

Let us make this plain. If one is not attracting good into his life there is something wrong with his unconscious thinking. The subjective state of his thought is wrong. The subjective state of thought constitutes the sum total of his belief. It is his habitual attitude toward life and living. This inner thought content is the sole medium between the absolute and the relative, between causes and conditions.

When this *inner* thought is clarified, that is, when it knows the truth, it will reinstate the outer man in peace, poise, health, and happiness. This inner thought becomes clarified as we unify with good; *this* is the inner quickening. Following this is the outer quickening, the outward sign of the inner belief.

When a man has this inner light he passes from death unto life. And this life unto which he passes is the life of God, consequently it is everlasting life. Death has nothing to do with life everlasting and is but an impatient gesture of the soul, wishing to rid itself of a body no longer useful.

THE WORD OF POWER

As the Father has life so the son has life. Again we have the teaching that there is but One Life, Mind, or Spirit. This Life is now our life and manifests through us as we believe in it. When our word is spoken in this consciousness of life, power, and action, then our word is life, power, and action. But of ourselves we cannot do this. That is, if we have a sense of isolation from the universe our word cannot bear the same fruit as it does when we realize the unity of life with our word.

The word has power only as it is one with power. Literally the word has no power of itself. The word is a mold which decides what form the thought is to take as it assumes shape and becomes a part of our conditions. Mental treatment is for the purpose of forming the word into such shapes and designs as are desirable for experience.

The word gives form to the unformed. The greater the consciousness behind the word the more power it will have. Just words, without conviction, have no power, and just conviction, without words, will never stir up latent energy. There must be a combination of the two to make a complete thing.

We are surrounded by a spiritual consciousness and a mental law. From combinations of these two, all things are made. We unify with the spiritual consciousness as we become aware of it. We speak it into form as we believe in the power of our own word. In treatment there should be first a realization of power, then a spoken word. One generates, the other distributes.

Labor not for the meat which perisheth, but for that meat
which endureth unto everlasting life, which the Son of
man shall give unto you:
For him hath God the Father sealed.
Verily, verily, I say unto you, Moses gave you not that bread
from heaven:
But my Father giveth you the true bread from heaven.
And Jesus said unto them, I am the bread of life: he that
cometh to me shall never hunger;
And he that believeth on me shall never thirst.
This is that bread which came down from heaven: not as your
fathers did eat manna, and are dead:
He that eateth of this bread shall live for ever.
It is the Spirit that quickeneth; the flesh profiteth nothing:
The words that I speak unto you, they are spirit, and they are
life.

JOHN 6

THE MEAT WHICH PERISHETH

"Labor not for the meat which perisheth." Jesus knew that we need
food to eat while in the flesh so he could not be referring to literal
food, but rather to that inner substance which is spiritual.

Starvation takes place on more than one plane. More people are
starved spiritually and intellectually than physically. A full stomach
will never appease an appetite for learning nor can a loaf of bread
satisfy the inner craving for reality. The *whole being* needs to be fed.

Bread and meat for the body, knowledge and wisdom for the soul, atmosphere and consciousness for the Spirit.

We live on three planes at the same time and always shall. To attempt to desert any one of these to the cost of the others is abnormal. To live only on the physical plane is to become a brute. To live only on the intellectual plane might produce a learned and a scientific man, but he would be only a mental machine. To live only on the spiritual plane might cause one to become a dreamer without any practical side to his nature.

THE THREE PLANES OF LIFE

Man is a threefold principle of life and action; he is spirit, soul, and body. From the spirit he receives inspiration and guidance, in the soul he finds a perfect law of life, and through the body he proves that he is a real individualization of the invisible principle.

Man's mind should swing from inspiration to action, from contemplation to accomplishment, from prayer to performance. This would be a well-balanced existence. The Spirit fires the soul with energy and understanding; the soul, which is the subjective mentality, vitalizes the body and animates all that we do.

No greater mistake could be made than to think we must separate life from what it does; we must unify and not divide. The Spirit must go forth into creation through law and action. Life must enter living and God must flow through man if there is to be a real representation of the divine through the human.

Let us feel that our purposes are animated and inspired from on high and then, let us go forth and make our dream come true in human experience. With an invisible Intelligence to guide, and an immutable Law to direct, let us take our place in any legitimate activity and thus cause our dreams to come to full fruition.

• •
•

> I am the light of the world: he that followeth me shall not walk in darkness, but shall have the light of life.
>
> If ye continue in my word, then are ye my disciples indeed;
>
> And ye shall know the truth, and the truth shall make you free.
>
> Verily, verily, I say unto you, If a man keep my saying, he shall never see death.

JOHN 8

• •
•

THE LIGHT OF THE WORLD

"I am the light of the world." Jesus was not referring to his human personality, but to the principle inherent in generic man. They who follow this inner principle shall have the light of life; for this principle is life.

"I Am" has a dual meaning. It is both individual and universal. God was revealed to Moses as the great "I Am," the universal Cause, the Causeless or self-existent One. Moses taught that "I Am" is the First Principle of all life, and the law of cause and effect running through everything. The whole teaching of Moses is based upon the perception of this "First Principle."

Jesus said that he came, not to destroy the law of Moses, but to fulfill it. How could he fulfill it except by teaching the relationship of the universal "I Am"—to the individual—I. In all the sayings of Jesus we find this thought brought out, that God is universal Spirit and man is His image and likeness, an individualization of His eternity.

Therefore, when we understand our own—"I"—we shall walk in that light which lights the world unto the perfect—"I Am."

We can consider this from another viewpoint. Man is the only self-knowing mind of which we are conscious; a self-knowing mind is conscious of what it knows. Man, the only self-conscious being in this world, must be the light of the world. To know this and to understand why it is so, is to know *that* truth which alone can make free. Truth is eternal and eternity is timeless, hence, if one knows the Truth he will never see death.

. .
.

A new commandment I give unto you, That ye love one another; as I have loved you, that ye also love one another.
By this shall all men know that ye are my disciples, if ye have
love one to another.

JOHN 13

. .
.

LOVE

Love is the central flame of the universe, nay, the very fire itself. It is written that God is Love and that we are the expressed likeness, the image of the Eternal Being. Love is self-givingness through creation, the impartation of the divine through the human.

Love is an essence, an atmosphere which defies analysis as does life itself. It is that which IS and cannot be explained: It is common to all people, to all animal life and evident in the response of plants to those who love them. Love reigns supreme over all.

The essence of love, while elusive, pervades everything, fires the heart, stimulates the emotions, renews the soul, and proclaims the spirit. Only love knows love, and love knows only love. Words cannot express its depths or meaning. A universal sense alone bears witness to the divine fact. God is Love and Love is God.

LOVE BALANCED BY LAW

Love, being the most subtle force known, the strongest latent energy, should be carefully preserved and guarded against the inroads of its opposite which is license. When the intellect decides that to which the emotions are to respond, then, love is balanced by law, but when the emotions are in the ascendency, chaos reigns with destruction following in its wake.

It is wrong to call emotional mistakes by the sacred name of love, thus attempting to dignify them by a false cloak. (See "Repression and Sublimation," *The Science of Mind*.) Love is pure in heart and sacred in its motives. It is the essence of goodness, spilled over everything and flowing through all.

It is easy to understand that God must be love, since everything in nature loves. Our love and our desire to express ourselves in terms of harmony and unity, is but a reflection of that Higher Mind, which is harmony and unity. Without love we are lost and with it there can be no loss.

THE EVOLUTION OF LOVE

The first love is that of the parent for its offspring; the outpouring of the mother and the givingness of the father. In this atmosphere the child is born into time and experience. Pressed from the creator into creation, in order that it may gain such knowledge as is necessary to develop a real individuality, the child comes from heaven or the central harmony.

The next love is that of the child for its parents. This is a reflection of their love to the child and when this reflection is free from care, burden and personal ownership, it is ever complete and satisfying.

The next love is that of the growing child for its playmates, a half affection, but of the essence of real love, for it is on equal terms. The community spirit is developing and this spirit is that of unity.

The next love is that of the grown child for its mate, the one chosen to be its companion in this life. This love is strong, true, virile, and assertive. It is the love of conquest, of personal adoration, of the melting of two souls into one life, and the reforming of this life on a basis of dual unity. From the fire of this passion and the union of these souls a new order of creation is to take place, and the old order of evolution is to be carried on.

A few steps beyond this love, the mind attuned to the real meaning of life, must reach out and love all humanity. This is the return journey of love, back to the central flame again; as the greater always includes the lesser, so the broader love includes the individual form which it has taken, for those who love humanity most, love their own immediate families and friends the best.

LOVE NECESSARY TO LIFE

Without love there is no hope of growth. The soul, unloving, becomes unlovely. Love is the giving of the self and without this flow there is no growth, no ripening of the finest force known in all nature.

Love itself is the universal urge of Spirit for self-expression and when this is stifled in the individual, life cannot express its greater good through him. Love always tends toward unity and an harmonious accord with people and things. When two people really love each other they do not quarrel, they unify. When a family, individually and collectively, loves its members, it remains in harmony and unity, and is bound together by a common interest and a common passion to preserve itself from all harm.

When the members of a community love one another that community is solid, prosperous, and happy. Nations are bound together by common interests and common affections. When the whole world realizes this it will unite in thought and in action. Love alone can solve the problems of international relations and bring about the day of universal peace.

• •
•

Let not your heart be troubled: ye believe in God, believe also in me.

In my Father's house are many mansions: if it were not so, I would have told you.

I go to prepare a place for you.

And if I go and prepare a place for you, I will come again, and receive you unto myself;

That where I am, there ye may be also.

And whither I go ye know, and the way ye know.

Thomas saith unto him, Lord, we know not whither thou goest; and how can we know the way?

Jesus saith unto him, I am the way, and the truth, and the life: No man cometh unto the Father, but by me.

If ye had known me, ye should have known my Father also: And from henceforth ye know him, and have seen him.

Philip saith unto him, Lord, shew us the Father, and it sufficeth us.

Jesus saith unto him, Have I been so long time with you, and yet hast thou not known me, Philip?

He that hath seen me hath seen the Father; and how sayest thou then, Shew us the Father?

Believest thou not that I am in the Father, and the Father in me?

The words that I speak unto you I speak not of myself: but the Father, that dwelleth in me, he doeth the works.

Believe me that I am in the Father, and the Father in me: Or else believe me for the very works' sake.

Verily, verily, I say unto you, He that believeth on me, the works that I do shall he do also;

And greater works than these shall he do; because I go unto my Father.

And whatsoever ye shall ask in my name, that will I do, that the Father may be glorified in the Son.

If ye shall ask any thing in my name, I will do it.

If ye love me, keep my commandments.

And I will pray the Father, and he shall give you another Comforter, that he may abide with you for ever;

Even the Spirit of truth; whom the world cannot receive, because it seeth him not, neither knoweth him:

But ye know him; for he dwelleth with you, and shall be in you.

At that day ye shall know that I am in my Father, and ye in me, and I in you.

He that hath my commandments, and keepeth them, he it is that loveth me:

And he that loveth me shall be loved of my Father, and I will love him, and will manifest myself to him.

These things have I spoken unto you, being yet present with you.

But the Comforter, which is the Holy Ghost, whom the Father will send in my name,

He shall teach you all things, and bring all things to your remembrance, whatsoever I have said unto you.

Peace I leave with you, my peace I give unto you: not as the world giveth, give I unto you.

Let not your heart be troubled, neither let it be afraid.

JOHN 14

. .
.

"LET NOT YOUR HEART
BE TROUBLED"

"Let not your heart be troubled; ye believe in God, believe also in me." His disciples were depressed, having an instinctive sense that Jesus was about to depart from them; they were filled with sadness. It was on the eve of his betrayal that he spoke these words, "Let not your heart be troubled," with that calm certainty, which has been given to the believing. He was not afraid. He had already plumbed the depths of human existence and penetrated into the beyond. He knew there is no death to the soul.

Our hearts are troubled over many things and our mental burdens often become unbearable. It seems, at times, as though a cup of bitterness were being held to unwilling lips, with the demand that they drink. Jesus, standing at the threshold of his greatest experience, foreknew that he would turn apparent defeat into glorious victory. From the calm depths of an undisturbed soul he spoke words of comfort to those of lesser understanding.

He told them to believe in God and because of their belief in God to believe also in him. Again he is referring to the individual—"I"—as the outward manifestation of the universal "I AM." We are to believe in ourselves because we believe in God. The two are ONE. We are to know that passing events cannot hinder the onward march of the soul. The temporal imperfection of the human cannot dim the eternal integrity of the Divine. The universe is to be trusted as are our best impulses. The best that is in us is God.

"IN MY FATHER'S HOUSE ARE MANY MANSIONS"

"In my Father's house are many mansions." This world, with all its wonders, is not the only one that we shall inhabit. There are many others and we shall inhabit each in time. If this life were the only life Jesus would have told his followers so. He held out no false promises, never deceived. He spoke only the Truth.

"I go to prepare a place for you." What more beautiful thought than that those who go before shall be there when we arrive! There is no death, only an expansion of the soul, an enlargement of the experience. But Thomas, who was a disciple, said that he did not know where Jesus was going nor did he know the way. Jesus answered, "I am the way, the truth and the life:" Again he is referring to the individual—"I"—the son of the eternal "I AM." This son is the way to the Father. We approach reality through our own natures and through no other source. "No man cometh unto the Father but by me." God is within and it is here that we meet Him. The inward gaze alone can reveal the Father.

WHO SEES THE SON
SEES THE FATHER

"He that hath seen me hath seen the Father." Many think, from this statement, that Jesus was claiming to be God, but such was not the case. God is the invisible Life Essence of all that is, the Intelligent Energy running through all. This life we feel but do not see. We see only what it does, never the thing itself.

Life manifests itself through the individual. Therefore, when one manifests goodness and purity he is revealing the Father. This is what Jesus meant when he said, "He that hath seen me hath seen the Father."

He said that his words were the words of God. As all forms of energy return again into their source, so the word of truth is the word of God, no matter who speaks it, or when it is spoken. Man reveals, but does not absorb the Divine Nature.

"He that believeth on me, the works that I do shall he do also." It could not be otherwise. The nature of reality was not exhausted in the man Jesus but made manifest through his life and works. We are to do likewise and what we ask in the name, which is our own name,

believing in the Father which is God, and in the Son, which is ourselves, we shall receive. In this way the Father is glorified in the Son.

THE HOLY COMFORTER

We are told that the Holy Comforter, the Spirit of Truth, will make
all things known unto us, for He is with us and in us. No more
comprehensive statement could be made. The Spirit of Truth is in
all people, not unto Jesus alone, but unto all alike, again the revelation of the self to the self; a divine awakening to the eternal reality
inhabiting eternity and finding its abiding place in time, through
our own natures.

As the Holy Comforter comes He makes all things known to us.
Intuition is the speech of this Comforter, instinct is His manner of
approach. "I am in my Father, and ye in me, and I in you." The eternal
Father begets the eternal Son; this son is generic and all are members
of this universal sonship. All are members of the one tree of life from
which every individual shoot springs. The Trinity is a Unity.

And that peace which comes from the innermost recesses of the
Spirit is left with us. A peace which the world cannot take away for it
springs from the bosom of the Father of light, love, life and wisdom.

⋅ ⋅
⋅

If ye abide in me, and my words abide in you, ye shall ask
what ye will, and it shall be done unto you.
Herein is my Father glorified, that ye bear much fruit; so
shall ye be my disciples.
As the Father hath loved me, so have I loved you: continue ye
in my love.

If ye keep my commandments, ye shall abide in my love;
even as I have kept my Father's commandments, and
abide in his love.

These things have I spoken unto you, that my joy might remain in you. And that your joy might be full.

This is my commandment, That ye love one another, as I have
loved you.

Greater love hath no man than this, that a man lay down his
life for his friends.

JOHN 15

ABIDING IN THE ONE

"If ye abide in me, and my words abide in you, ye shall ask what ye will, and it shall be done unto you."

As it is impossible for humanity to literally abide in the man Jesus we must look for a figurative meaning in these words. He is speaking of the spirit of his teachings; and the whole *spirit* of his teachings is to the effect that man is an individualized center of God-consciousness. The spirit of man is the Spirit of God, for God is One.

When we abide in the One we cannot ask amiss but must ask for that which is right and good, consequently our prayers to the One will be answered. But let us remember that prayer is answered according to law, and this law is one of liberty and never one of license. True liberty comes only through true harmony, true harmony only through true unity, and true unity can come only by the conscious realization that we are one with God or good.

Jesus says that it will be done unto us. He implies a power which can and will work for those who harmonize with, and believe in it. But we must first abide in the spirit of Truth. And what is the spirit of Truth other than that we live in conscious unity with good and do harm to no one. Goodness is natural while evil is abnormal.

To trust in the law of good is to constantly believe that we are surrounded by a power which can and will cast all fear from our minds, free us from all bondage, and set us safe and satisfied in a new order of living.

"THAT YE BEAR MUCH FRUIT"

"Herein is my Father glorified, that ye bear much fruit." When we express a greater livingness, then Life is more completely expressing itself through us. A barren tree does not express the principle of abundance and production, so a life barren of good works does not fully express the divine ideal.

Evolution has brought man to a point of self-expression and it can do no more for him until he consciously cooperates with it. Its law is one of growth and unfoldment. God goes forth anew into creation whenever anyone discovers a new truth or increases knowledge about an old one. Each is a center of the All, and each has access to the All, through his own nature.

Jesus refers to his joy on the eve of his greatest lesson to mankind. That joy which is full and complete. That joy which no man takes away. The joy of a sense of completion. He was about to lay down his earthly life as the greatest object lesson ever taught. And what was this lesson? That love knows no bounds and, the Eternal Goodness *gives all to all*.

For the invisible things of him from the creation of the world
   are clearly seen,
Being understood by the things that are made.

ROMANS 2

. .
.

THE LAW OF CORRESPONDENTS

This teaching incorporates the great law of correspondents. The
spiritual world contains an image of the physical; the physical is a
counterpart of the spiritual. A true estimate of the outward symbol
points to the spiritual reality behind it.

We understand the unseen by correctly viewing the seen. The
outward effect must partake of its inward nature. The physical universe is the result of an inner intelligence, working through the law

of matter, and molding it into many different forms. Behind form is idea.

In Religious Science we say there is a subjective cause for every objective effect. In psychology we say, the subjective mind is the builder of the body and creator of the circumstances. We go from the known to the unknown, no one sees causes, they remain forever hidden from the physical gaze, but the seen proves the unseen, the formless gives itself form through the creative power of its own mind and Spirit.

Behind every effect there is a cause, and if this cause is a spiritual idea, which it must be, then it follows that should the spiritual idea be discerned the physical effect would be like it. The entire possibility of demonstrating the law of good depends on this proposition. The idea is father to the fact. Ideas are real, having the power within themselves to be made manifest.

The whole teaching of the Bible is to the effect that God is universal Spirit, and universal creation. He creates by the power of His word; this word is the law of His being. Man reproduces the divine nature on the scale of the individual. He also uses creative power which works through the law of his word. From this he cannot escape, he need only use this power constructively and all will be well. If he uses the creative power of his thought destructively then it will destroy.

In Religious Science we learn that persistent, constructive thought is the greatest power known and the most effective.

If the visible effect in our lives is not what it should be, if we are unhappy, sick, and poverty stricken, we already know the remedy. The Truth is always the remedy, and the Truth *is* that the law of liberty is the only real law. When we reverse the process of thought the effect will be reversed.

. .
.

There is therefore now no condemnation to them, who walk
not after the flesh, but after the Spirit.

For the law of the Spirit . . . hath made me free from the law
of sin and death.

They that are after the flesh do mind the things of the flesh;

But they that are after the Spirit the things of the Spirit.

For to be carnally minded is death; but to be spiritually
minded is life and peace.

Because the carnal mind is enmity against God: for it is not
subject to the law of God, neither indeed can be.

If the Spirit of him that raised up Jesus from the dead dwell
in you,

He that raised up Christ from the dead shall also quicken
your mortal bodies by his Spirit that dwelleth in you.

For as many as are led by the Spirit of God, they are the sons
of God.

For ye have not received the Spirit of bondage again to fear;

But ye have received the Spirit of adoption, whereby we cry,
Abba, Father.

The Spirit itself beareth witness with our spirit, that we are
the children of God:

And if children, then heirs; heirs of God, and joint-heirs with
Christ;

If so be that we suffer with him, that we may be also glorified
together.

For I reckon that the sufferings of this present time are not
worthy to be compared with the glory which shall be revealed in us.

For the earnest expectation of the creature waiteth for the
manifestation of the sons of God.

Because the creature itself also shall be delivered from the
bondage of corruption into the glorious liberty of the
children of God.

And we know that all things work together for good to them
that love God, to them who are the called according to
his purpose.

For whom he did foreknow, he also did predestinate to be
conformed to the image of his Son.

What shall we then say to these things? If God be for us, who
can be against us?

Who shall separate us from the love of Christ? shall tribulation, or distress, or persecution, or famine, or nakedness,
or peril, or sword?

Nay, in all these things we are more than conquerors, through
him that loved us.

For I am persuaded, that neither death, nor life, nor angels,
nor principalities, nor powers, nor things present, nor
things to come,

Nor height, nor depth, nor any other creature, shall be able
to separate us from the love of God.

Romans 8

THERE IS NO CONDEMNATION

"There is therefore now no condemnation to them, who walk . . .
after the Spirit." As it is impossible for us to be in another man, and
as it is necessary that each live his own life, within the One Life, it

follows that the writer was not referring to a personality but to a universal principle.

We are in Christ when we are in the Truth; we are in the Truth when we live in harmony with it; there is no mystery about this, it is common sense. The law of the Spirit makes us free from sin and death: the law of the Spirit is freedom and knows no bondage. When we enter the Spirit we come under its law of freedom.

Sin means mistake, or missing the mark. We miss the mark when we do not live under the law of harmony, which is Truth. From mistakes come the experience of death. Death is no part of eternal life, which can know no death, so it follows that God knows nothing about death. We die from one plane to another until we learn how to live. This is good and necessary and is the only way we could learn the lesson of life, which must be learned by all before real freedom can come.

"To be spiritually minded is life and peace." Who does not long for life and peace? These are contained in the Spirit, which is the center and circumference of all. The carnal mind is not subject to the law of God because it is a limited concept of Truth. The carnal mind symbolizes anything that disbelieves in the supremacy of Good; it is a belief in isolation, a sense of separation from good.

THE SPIRIT THAT RAISED JESUS

The Spirit that raised Jesus dwells in all; this Spirit quickens our mortal bodies when we let it. Here is a lesson in mental and spiritual healing. As the Truth dawns upon the subjective state of our thought it stimulates it into newness of action and fresh outline.

Everything works from within out. The body is a reflection of the soul and when the soul, which is the subjective state of thought, is illumined by the Spirit, it quickens the mortal part of us and heals the body. The mortal is always an effect, a creature of time but a necessary one, for without it we could not function as individuals.

THE SPIRIT OF ADOPTION

We have not received a spirit of bondage but one of adoption. This is a mystical and beautiful saying. It implies that we are adopted by the Supreme Spirit as Its own offspring. How could it be otherwise since we are made of the same stuff as the central fire. There is no fear in the Spirit and there will be none in us when we realize who and what we are. God wishes us well and knows only that we are now free and perfect. This is the spirit of freedom whereby we are all born free.

JOINT HEIRS WITH CHRIST

The inner Spirit, which is God, bears witness to the divine fact that we are the sons of God, the children of the Most High. As sons of God we are heirs to the heaven of reality; joint heirs with Christ. This means that we are all one in Christ as we are one in God. Christ typifies the universal Son of which each is an individual member.

Our expectation looks for a more complete manifestation of our own inner divinity. Evolution will bring this about as it does all things. We are an unfolding principle of life, truth, perfect law, and action. We wait for a more complete unfolding of our inner life. It is already within, the perfect way and the eternal Truth. We wait for the unfolding of ourselves, through the law inherent within our real nature.

THE INNER LIGHT

The creature shall be delivered from bondage. As the inner light dawns it delivers the outer life from bondage. This is in line with the teaching that everything is from within out. When the *soul* knows freedom the *law* will free the body and the outer life will express health, happiness, and success.

All things work for our good. Even that which we call evil is salutary, leading us to the Way, the Truth, and the Life. Suffering should teach us a lesson which would cause us to refrain from making more mistakes; it carries a blessing with it when we learn how to learn.

PREDESTINATION

"For whom he did foreknow, he also did predestinate." God foreknows His own perfection and the perfection of His entire creation, so it is foreknown and predetermined by the Divine Mind that all shall be sons of God. Man cannot forever keep himself from his birthright; all will eventually be saved from themselves—as there can be no such thing as eternal damnation. To believe in such an absurd doctrine is worse than ignorance. Emerson tells us that there is no sin but ignorance.

God knows only perfection; when we know as God knows, our troubles will be rolled up like a scroll and numbered with past illusions.

GOD'S WILL FOR HIS CREATION

"If God be for us, who can be against us?" If God is all there is and if the universe is One, then there is no power, presence or law against the Truth. One with the Truth is a totality. But we should be careful to be on the side of Truth. If our whole endeavor is to be, and to do, that which is constructive, then we are with God and we may be sure that He is ever with us. God knows no outside. He is ever inside. The outer rim of reality is exactly at the center of itself.

Nothing can keep us from the love of God. What comfort! What joy, to know that all is well with the soul! What untold sufferings we have had because of our doubts and fears! And we are told not to be afraid, for it is the Father's good pleasure to give us the Kingdom. Man alone has tried to rob us of our birthright—the glorious liberty of the Sons of the Most High.

Let us honor God more, and man less. Let us seek within for the cause; it can be found in no other place. There is nothing that can keep us from this inner vision of the eternal reality.

∴

I beseech you therefore, brethren, by the mercies of God,
that ye present your bodies a living sacrifice, holy, acceptable unto God, which is your reasonable service.

And be not conformed to this world; but be ye transformed by the renewing of your mind.

That ye may prove what is that good, and acceptable, and perfect will of God.

For as we have many members in one body, and all members have not the same office;

So we, being many, are one body in Christ, and everyone members of another.

Having then gifts differing according to the grace that is given to us, whether prophecy, let us prophesy according to the proportion of faith;

Or ministry, let us wait on our ministering; or he that teacheth, on teaching.

Or he that exhorteth, on exhortation: he that giveth, let him do it with simplicity;

He that ruleth, with diligence; he that showeth mercy, with cheerfulness.

Let love be without dissimulation. Abhor that which is evil; cleave to that which is good.

Be kindly affectioned one to another with brotherly love; in honor preferring one another;

Not slothful in business; fervent in spirit; serving the Lord;

Rejoicing in hope; patient in tribulation, continuing instant in prayer;

Bless them which persecute you; bless, and curse not.

Be of the same mind one toward another.

Mind not high things, but condescend to men of low estate.

Be not wise in your own conceits.

Recompense to no man evil for evil.

Provide things honest in the sight of all men.

If it be possible, as much as lieth in you, live peaceably with
all men.

Dearly beloved, avenge not yourselves, but rather give place
unto wrath:

For it is written, Vengeance is mine; I will repay, saith the Lord.

Therefore if thine enemy hunger, feed him; if he thirst, give
him drink:

For in so doing thou shalt heap coals of fire on his head.

Be not overcome of evil, but overcome evil with good.

ROMANS 12

. .
.

THE RENEWING OF THE MIND

"Be ye transformed by the renewing of your mind." Today we know
what this means. The renewing of the mind is a scientific act. As the
conscious thought pours truth into the subjective channels of creative energy, the body is automatically renewed; this is mental healing. Mental healing is a conscious act as well as an established fact in
the experience of many people. Instead of the old concepts of disease and failure we are to inject those of liberty, freedom, health,
harmony, and success.

Mental healing is subject to the exact laws of mind and Spirit, and
is accomplished by correct knowing. This knowing is a mental attitude toward the Truth. It is the *Truth* that makes free, and it is the
mind which knows the Truth. (See "Mental Healing," *Science of Mind.*)

The body is healed as the inner mind is transformed; as the old
and false images of thought are renewed by images of truth and life.

The process through which this renewing takes place is a conscious one and may be practiced by any who understands the principle involved.

"BLESS AND CURSE NOT"

"Bless, and curse not." Here is the whole law and prophets. We are to overcome evil with good. Evil lasts but for a day while goodness shines to eternity and loving kindness is the very nature of Deity. As the darkness has no power over light, so evil is overcome with good.

"Vengeance is mine; I will repay, saith the Lord." This is a statement of the law of cause and effect. *God* does not avenge but the law of cause and effect exacts the uttermost farthing; we need not worry how things are coming out; the law takes care of everything and returns to each exactly what is his due.

· ·
·

Let every soul be subject unto the higher powers. For there is no power but of God: the powers that be are ordained of God.

Owe no man anything, but to love one another: for he that loveth another hath fulfilled the law.

Love worketh no ill to his neighbor: therefore love is the fulfilling of the law.

And that, knowing the time, that now it is high time to awake out of sleep:

For now is our salvation nearer than when we believed.

The night is far spent, the day is at hand: let us therefore cast
off the works of darkness, and let us put on the armor of
light.

ROMANS 13

THE GREAT AWAKENING

"Now it is high time to awake out of sleep." The belief in a life apart
from Good is a dream from which we must awake if we are to taste
the waters of reality, which flow from the source of life.

As one awakes from a nightmare, so the mentality awakes from
the dream of a living death to a realization of eternal life. We cast
off the works of darkness when we realize that evil is not an entity
but a fraud. The armor of light is the Truth, the very knowing of
which makes free.

This awakening is a process of evolution, a little here and a little
there until the whole eye is opened and we see that life is neither
separate from God nor different from Good. Life is God, and
Good is the only power there is, or can be.

To awaken to oneself is to be healed, made prosperous, happy,
and satisfied; to be made every whit whole; to become complete as
we were intended to be. God is a God of the living and not of the
dead. He sees and knows only perfection and completion; happiness and satisfaction. When we shall think of ourselves as *God*
knows us, then complete salvation will have come to us.

Who art thou that judgest another man's servant? to his own
master he standeth or falleth.

Yea, he shall be holden up; for God is able to make him
stand.

One man esteemeth one day above another: another esteemeth every day alike.

Let every man be fully persuaded in his own mind.

None of us liveth to himself, and no man dieth to himself.

For to this end Christ both died, and rose, and revived, that
he might be Lord both of the dead and living.

Let us not therefore judge one another any more: but judge
this rather,

That no man put a stumbling block, or an occasion to fall, in
his brother's way.

I know, and am persuaded by the Lord Jesus, that there is
nothing unclean of itself:

But to him that esteemeth any thing to be unclean, to him it
is unclean.

Let us therefore follow after the things which make for
peace, and things wherewith one may edify another.

Hast thou faith? have it to thyself before God.

Happy is he that condemneth not himself in that thing which
he alloweth.

And he that doubteth is damned if he eat, because he eateth
not of faith: for whatsoever is not of faith is sin.

ROMANS 14

· ·
·

"THERE IS NOTHING
UNCLEAN OF ITSELF"

"Let every man be fully persuaded in his own mind." The writer was a clear-thinking man; he knew that God does not esteem one day above another. Had not Jesus already said that the Sabbath was made for man and not man for the Sabbath? In all such matters the only criterion is our own judgment. That which our own consciousness makes clear *is* clear, and this inner guide plus reason, will reveal Truth to anyone.

God knows nothing about outward forms and ceremonies. The inner parts must be made clean and receptive to the Divine Influx, nothing else matters.

"There is nothing unclean of itself." Here is a great lesson: *things,* of themselves, are not unclean, although we often make them so: to the pure all is pure, to the clean all is clean; a clean mind will manifest in a clean body and environment. The law of cause and effect again.

We are to follow that which makes for peace and with peace in our minds we shall find peace wherever we go. The man who does not condemn that which he does, is happy; here is a practical lesson in the science of psychology. When we do that which the inner light forbids, we create complexes on the subjective side of life which irritate the inner thought, producing confusion in everything we do.

If psychology has taught us anything it has taught that we cannot think one way and act another without confusion. When the emotions are in conflict with the intellect and the will, disastrous results follow.

The way to avoid confusion is to think and act clearly. This alone would heal many of our diseases. Whatsoever is not of faith is sin, or a mistake. Sin means making a mistake or missing the mark.

A careful self-analysis is good for all. We should keep the inner mind clear by never contradicting our highest values or compromising with our emotions. A false thought can be consciously removed by a true one; thus complexes are removed from the mind through right thinking.

We should never condemn ourselves or others and never allow others to condemn us. That to which the mind reacts affirmatively will appear to be true to the one believing it, even though it be erroneous. The law is no respecter of persons and will act as law in each and every case.

.·.

But we speak the wisdom of God in a mystery, even the hidden wisdom, which God ordained before the world.

But as it is written, Eye hath not seen, nor ear heard, neither have entered into the heart of man,

The things which God hath prepared for them that love him.

But God hath revealed them unto us by his Spirit: for the Spirit searcheth all things, yea, the deep things of God.

For what man knoweth the things of man, save the spirit of man which is in him?

Even so the things of God knoweth no man, but the Spirit of God.

Now we have received, not the spirit of the world, but the spirit which is of God;

That we might know the things that are freely given to us of God.

Which things also we speak, not in the words which man's
wisdom teacheth, but which the Holy Ghost teacheth;
comparing spiritual things with spiritual.

But the natural man receiveth not the things of the Spirit of
God:

For they are foolishness unto him: neither can he know
them, because they are spiritually discerned.

But he that is spiritual judgeth all things, yet he himself is
judged of no man.

For who hath known the mind of the Lord, that he may instruct him?

But we have the mind of Christ.

I CORINTHIANS 2

SYMBOLS

When Paul says that he speaks the wisdom of God in a mystery, he
is in line with the teaching of his time. In the old religious orders
there was an exoteric and an esoteric teaching. The esoteric for the
inner circles and the exoteric for the outer. The people were given
symbols, but only the priests and perhaps a few others knew the
meaning of the symbol. To the common people the knowledge of
God was a mystery; a hidden wisdom. Wisdom is always hidden
since we do not see it, but we can *understand* much of that which we
do not *see*.

In our age the symbol is no longer necessary for we know its
meaning. For instance, the bread and wine of the Lord's Supper
symbolize that we live in a universe of Spirit and of Substance. We

know the meaning of the symbol, and knowing its meaning can dispense with the symbol.

INTUITION

Eye hath not seen the glories of the universe in which we live but they have been revealed by the Spirit. The Spirit in us, which is the Spirit of God, makes these things known through intuition, by reason, and through divine revelation. But we must compare spiritual things with spiritual. To be spiritually minded is to understand the Spirit.

We have received the Spirit of God and know the things that are of the Spirit. This statement means that our spirit is the Spirit of God and by this Spirit we know Truth. The intuitive faculty is the mind of God, in us, differing from the universal Mind only in degree.

The natural man cannot receive the things of Spirit because they are foolishness to him. Intuition is a direct perception of truth without the process of reasoning; it does not transcend reason itself for it is a perception of the original reason of all.

We cannot instruct God but we do have the mind of Christ. The mind of Christ is the spiritual perception through which we perceive truth. The mind of Christ is the mind of God in us and needs no instruction. It is the *outer* mind that needs instruction; the mind of Christ already knows.

⁖

Every man shall receive his own reward, according to his own labor.

We are laborers together with God: ye are God's husbandry, ye are God's building.

If any man's work abide which he hath built thereupon, he shall receive a reward.

If any man's work shall be burnt, he shall suffer loss: but he himself shall be saved; yet so as by fire.

Know ye not that ye are the temple of God, and that the Spirit of God dwelleth in you?

Let no man deceive himself. If any man among you seemeth to be wise in this world, let him become a fool, that he may be wise.

For the wisdom of this world is foolishness with God.

For it is written, He taketh the wise in their own craftiness.

Whether Paul, or Apollos, or Cephas, or the world, or life, or death, or things present or things to come; all are yours;

And ye are Christ's; and Christ is God's.

I CORINTHIANS 3

. .
.

THE BELIEF IN ETERNAL
DAMNATION IS MADNESS

Any work which is of the Truth receives a reward. The law of compensation looks after this as it does after everything else. If any man's work be burnt, that is, if it is not of the Truth, he will suffer loss but the man himself will be saved. Paul knew that there is no eternal damnation to the soul. He said that when we make mistakes we suffer as by fire. He does not say that we suffer by fire, but, "as by fire," the stricken consciousness, the sense that we might have done better. The burning of the dross from the soul is, "as by fire," but the man himself will be saved. In the end all will reach the same goal; to believe otherwise would be madness.

Man is the temple of God and the Holy Spirit indwells every soul. When the outer temple is unfit it is destroyed; but it is evident that if the inmate is the Spirit of God It cannot be destroyed, even by the greatest of human foolishness. The embodiment may be destroyed and is, but the inner temple itself, that structure reared on the foundations of the universe, is eternal. That which is mortal of us will perish but that which is immortal *is immortal.*

To believe in any form of eternal damnation is sheer madness. Whatever man is, he is because he IS, and since he did not make himself he cannot help being what he is. But he does not yet manifest his true nature and much that he now manifests will be done away with, while that which is real will live forever.

"AND YE ARE CHRIST'S; AND CHRIST IS GOD'S"

"All things are yours; and ye are Christ's; and Christ is God's." Here we have three beings, ourselves, Christ and God; and we are Christ's and Christ is God's. The human is an offshoot of the divine, the divine is an offshoot of the Absolute Itself. Humanity is what we see, Christ is the divine man, God is the Father of all.

The body has a life in matter, the soul has a life in mind and mind has a life in the Spirit. The principle of life ascends from the external to the highest internal and descends from the highest innermost to the lowest outermost. This teaching is as old as time.

．．
．

Now there are diversities of gifts, but the same Spirit.

And there are differences of administrations, but the same Lord.

And there are diversities of operations, but it is the same God which worketh all in all.

But the manifestation of the Spirit is given to every man to profit withal.

For to one is given by the Spirit the word of wisdom; to another the word of knowledge by the same Spirit.

To another faith by the same Spirit; to another the gifts of healing by the same Spirit;

To another the working of miracles; to another prophecy; to another discerning of spirits; to another divers kinds of tongues; to another the interpretation of tongues;

But all these worketh that one and the self-same Spirit, dividing to every man severally as he will.

For as the body is one and hath many members, and all the members of that one body, being many, are one body; so also is Christ.

For by one Spirit are we all baptized into one body, whether we be bond or free;

And have been all made to drink into one Spirit.

I Corinthians 12

．．
．

MANY GIFTS BUT ONE SPIRIT

There are many gifts but one Spirit; many operations but one Operator! This teaching is self-evident. There is a perfect Unit behind everything. This original One is the cause of all that follows. The outer is the result of the inner. The inner is One, the outer is many—in order that the One may be expressed.

The problem of philosophy is to reconcile the necessary unit to its multiplied effects. We live in a world of things, time, happenings, and passing events. All this takes place within the One.

Let us consider the element of time. Time is the measure of an event: it is a sequence of events in that which is a unitary whole. God is timeless, that is, He exists from eternity to eternity. Things come and go. God, the Timeless, enters time in order that He may be expressed. Without time there could be no expression of the Timeless, therefore, time is as necessary to God as to man.

We will now consider matter. All material forms come from one original substance which is the stuff of every diversified form. One substance but many forms. Unless this one substance were broken into many forms, the formless could not be expressed; and as it is the nature of Being to be expressed, there must be different forms; many operations but one Operator.

There are many spirits, but only one Spirit; many personalities but only one universal Person. Many men but one God. No one man completely expresses the Infinite; each expresses some gift of the higher life; all, together, comprise generic man, which is Christ. All are members of Christ as branches; all belong to one trunk. And Christ is God's.

"All made to drink into one Spirit." All derive life from the one source of life. All drink from one fountain and since this is the fountain of life Itself there is enough and to spare. Each takes what he can hold. He *cannot* take more.

We are all of one body. The entire creation is the body of the Infinite. Each is an individual member of this one body, "by one Spirit we are all baptized into one body."

. .
.

> Though I speak with the tongues of men and of angels, and have not charity, I am become as sounding brass, or a tinkling cymbal.
>
> And though I have the gift of prophecy, and understand all mysteries, and all knowledge;
>
> And though I have all faith, so that I could remove mountains, and have not charity, I am nothing.
>
> Charity suffereth long, and is kind; charity envieth not; charity vaunteth not itself, is not puffed up.
>
> Doth not behave itself unseemly, seeketh not her own, is not easily provoked, thinketh no evil;
>
> Rejoiceth not in iniquity, but rejoiceth in the truth;
>
> Beareth all things, believeth all things, hopeth all things, endureth all things.
>
> Charity never faileth: but whether there be prophecies, they shall fail; whether there be tongues, they shall cease; whether there be knowledge, it shall vanish away.
>
> For we know in part, and we prophesy in part.
>
> But when that which is perfect is come, then that which is in part shall be done away.
>
> When I was a child, I spake as a child, I understood as a child, I thought as a child;
>
> But when I became a man, I put away childish things.
>
> For now we see through a glass darkly; but then face to face:

Now I know in part; but then shall I know even as also I am known.

And now abideth faith, hope, charity, these three; but the greatest of these is charity.

I Corinthians 13

• •
•

LOVE CANNOT FAIL

This is one of the most beautiful chapters in the Bible. Though we speak with the tongue of an angel and have not love, we miss the mark. Though we give many things to the poor but withhold the giver we give nothing. "The gift without the giver is bare."

Charity, or love, cannot fail. Jesus said that to those who love much, much will be forgiven. "Love never faileth." Paul says that though we are able to move mountains and have not love we do not accomplish. Everything human shall pass away, but love will forever remain the chief cornerstone of reality.

NOW WE SEE IN PART

Now we know only in part and see only in part, but the perfect vision is dawning and we shall yet see, know and experience, that which we now know only through the inner sense. "Now we see through a glass darkly."

In the invisible world there are many things which do not yet appear. Evolution is the eternal manifestation of the more yet to come. Whatever life is, or shall be, it always has been, in potentiality—the apparent more is but the unfolding of our own consciousness. Evolution, on this or any other planet, is a continuous manifestation of an inner life, constantly expanding and expressing in an objective state.

.　.
　.

Let him that speaketh in an unknown tongue pray that he
　　may interpret.
For if I pray in an unknown tongue, my spirit prayeth, but my
　　understanding is unfruitful.
What is it then? I will pray with the spirit, and I will pray
　　with the understanding also;
I will sing with the spirit, and I will sing with the under-
　　standing also.
I had rather speak five words with my understanding, that by
　　my voice I might teach others also,
Than ten thousand words in an unknown tongue.
Brethren, be not children in understanding: howbeit in mal-
　　ice be ye children, but in understanding be men.
For God is not the author of confusion, but of peace.
Let all things be done decently and in order.

I Corinthians 14

.　.
　.

NOT CONFUSION BUT PEACE

Paul tells us that he would rather speak a few words with understanding than many words in an unknown tongue. "For God is not the author of confusion, but of peace." In the early days of the church many had visions and spoke in "unknown tongues," and they often labored under psychic hallucinations.

When God speaks He uses a language which can be understood and not one of confusion. But when one is in a psychic state he is subject to the influences of many powers and confusion follows. The Bible is filled with warnings against the wrong use of this power. We should not shut our eyes to the fact that there are more things in this world than are seen with the physical eye.

Thousands speak in "unknown tongues" today and many are misled thereby. We are to subject all such experiences to the test of reason, which is the "understanding." If an apparent revelation contradicts the rule of reason, then we are not speaking the truth and confusion follows. We are speaking in an "unknown tongue" and not from the inspiration of God, who is the author of peace.

The psychic life is but little understood and therefore subject to much misuse. When we enter the subjective world, letting go the objective faculties of discrimination, we are in danger of receiving impressions that are not true or healthful. It is a mistake to surrender the faculties of reason to the confusion of false suggestions.

In the subjective world we are surrounded by thought pictures and mental vibrations of various kinds, some good and some not good. The only safe way to enter this field of mind, is with the eyes open and the objective faculties on the alert. "Who breaketh through an hedge, a serpent shall bite him."

We are in an age when the subjective faculties are rapidly developing. This is necessary to the evolution of the individual or it would not be so. But few understand the subjective life and the reaction of thought to unconscious impressions. Much which is thought to be inspiration or revelation is but subjective hallucination.

We must carefully study all claims to revelation and see if they keep faith with reason. If they do not they must be false. When one is in a subjective state he might see images of thought and mistake them for realities; he might see the image of a departed soul and mistake this image for the person himself. This is a mistake very common to the average psychic and one which should be carefully avoided.

No mental state is normal when not under control of the conscious faculties. God is not the author of confusion.

. .
.

By man came death, by man came also the resurrection of
the dead.

For as in Adam all die, even so in Christ shall all be made
alive.

The last enemy that shall be destroyed is death.

But some man will say, How are the dead raised up? and with
what body do they come?

There are celestial bodies, and bodies terrestrial: but the
glory of the celestial is one, and the glory of the terrestrial is another.

So also is the resurrection of the dead. It is sown in corruption; it is raised in incorruption:

It is sown in dishonor; it is raised in glory; it is sown in weakness; it is raised in power:

It is sown a natural body, it is raised a spiritual body.

There is a natural body, and there is a spiritual body.

And so it is written, The first man Adam was made a living
soul; the last Adam was a quickening spirit.

Howbeit that was not first which is spiritual, but that which
is natural; and afterward that which is spiritual.

The first man is of the earth, earthy; the second man is the
Lord from heaven.

As is the earthy, such are they also that are earthy; and as is
the heavenly, such are they also that are heavenly.

And as we have borne the image of the earthy, we shall also
bear the image of the heavenly.

Now this I say, brethren, that flesh and blood cannot inherit
the kingdom of God;

Neither doth corruption inherit incorruption.

Behold, I shew you a mystery; We shall not all sleep, but we
shall all be changed.

For this corruptible must put on incorruption, and this mortal must put on immortality.

So when this corruptible shall have put on incorruption, and
this mortal shall have put on immortality,

Then shall be brought to pass the saying that is written,

Death is swallowed up in victory.

O death, where is thy sting? O grave, where is thy victory?

I CORINTHIANS 15

DEATH AND THE RESURRECTION

"By man came death, by man also came the resurrection." Here is a
plain statement that man alone is responsible for death and the resurrection. The great teacher has told us, "God is not the God of the
dead but of the living, for all live unto Him."

Through our mistakes we die. All die in Adam, and all are made
alive in Christ. Christ and Adam are two different names for the
same man; one is earthly, the other is heavenly. Adam typifies the
material man with his false estimate of life, while Christ typifies

the principle of holiness, or wholeness. Each of us is both Adam and Christ. We die daily in Adam and daily are we resurrected in Christ. There is a daily death to that which is untrue and a daily rebirth into the true.

The angel of our better selves keeps watch by the graves of our lesser selves, pointing the way to life, truth, and beauty. This angel is Christ, forever dwelling in the bosom of the eternal Spirit. Adam pulls down; Christ uplifts.

By man alone came mistakes. By man alone will come salvation. Let us remember the saying of Emerson: "The finite alone has wrought and suffered, the Infinite lies stretched in smiling repose." The finite must put on the Infinite if it is to be resurrected. The resurrection principle is the eternal manifestation of life in higher and higher forms of expression.

Man fell. Man will have to rise. God will never desert him but will ever manifest Himself to any who consciously partakes of the Divine Nature. We are to look, not to the fallen Adam, but to the resurrected Christ. Both are within us.

THE LAST ENEMY

Death is the last enemy to be destroyed. Paul believed death could be done away with. What is death but a greater claim which the soul makes upon the deathless principle of life? Physical death is occasioned by the inability of the soul to longer function through the body. It is a release which comes when the body is no longer a fit instrument for the functioning soul. The soul will not forever be limited. It instinctively knows its own freedom.

Death is no part of life, and eternal life knows no death. We shall know death as long as we contradict eternal life. When we shall completely learn the lesson of life, death will be overcome. The dawning of this day no man knows, but that it is certain to come is evident if life is immortal.

THERE ARE EARTHLY AND HEAVENLY BODIES

Paul tells us there are earthly bodies and heavenly bodies and that the earthly must put on the heavenly. This is in line with the teaching that we die from one plane to another and will, until the lesson of life is learned. This teaching is reasonable and acceptable to all who think the problem out to its logical conclusion.

When we stand beside the bier of a loved one, our hearts cannot but be filled with sorrow because of the physical absence of our beloved: yet our souls are filled with holy awe at the marvelous transformation which he has undergone. The mortal has become more aware of immortality. The human has expanded more greatly into the divine. Our loved one has passed to a greater recognition of life, truth, and beauty.

It is but natural that we grieve, and we would not wish it otherwise, for the most beautiful thing in life is personal love and friendship. This is the most Godlike attribute of human existence. When a loved one passes from among us we grieve, for an empty place will be left, but we know that with the dawn of that eternal morning his face will again be seen, and again we shall clasp his hand.

Our grief is lost in joy when we realize that our beloved has but gone before; that life is eternal, forever expanding into more beautiful forms for the expression of the incarnated God who indwells every soul. The spirit of man is a spark of the Infinite Fire of Life, caught in human mold. It is a drop of the Infinite Ocean and must return to its source.

The passing of the human body is necessary to the evolution of the soul and when, by reason of sickness, accident, or infirmity, it is no longer a fit instrument through which the incarnating spirit may work it is laid aside that this spirit, which knows itself to be free, may expand and express. When the soul needs a new body through which to function it takes one.

THE EXPANSION OF THE SOUL

And so, in a certain sense, we rejoice at the experience which has come to our friend. He is now enjoying a more abundant life, in a body more perfect, a home more heavenly. He has come closer to the great Heart of all. He has passed through the portals of mortality and is more conscious of eternity; he is the guest of God.

But his memory shall be to us as sweet rosemary, as the incense of heaven, the gift of God. And this memory shall still be fresh when we meet again on those shores of life everlasting from whose boundaries men do not depart. And ever shall this memory uplift, help, and guide us on the roadway which we are traveling. We feel that we have not lost our friend, for he still dwells in the home of our thought, he still lives in our hearts, and in the book of mind his face is still seen and known. The beauty of his strength, the sympathy of his presence and the love of his heart are ours forever.

The gift of God is returned to Him only in part, for there has been left behind the sweet radiance of an earthly life, well lived and well loved.

THE SOUL IS INDEPENDENT OF THE BODY

That the soul is independent of the body is proven by the very fact of death itself; for, when the soul leaves it, the body at once begins to disintegrate—because the life principle has deserted it. It is evident that something real has left, for until now the body has responded to some subtle power which is not physical. If the body, itself, could act, it would continue to do so. The body cannot act, it is acted through; it has been a vehicle for the functioning soul, but is now a garment no more fitting: it is thrown aside to return to the dust from which it sprang, while the Spirit returns to the God who gave it.

What is an individual? What is a Man? He is a center of conscious life, intelligence, and action, equipped with choice, volition, and free thought. What attributes does he possess which enable him to make use of these powers while on earth? Those which we call the senses; and yet we could not take from him any one of them. If the eye could see, it would keep on seeing; if the brain could think it would think on and on forever.

Paul tells us there is another eye behind the physical one, that there is a thinker back of thought, using the brain as a physical vehicle while man is clothed in flesh. And when, by reason of physical inadequacy, the brain is no longer a good instrument the thinker quietly deserts it and takes a new one.

PSYCHOLOGICAL PROOF
OF IMMORTALITY

Psychological investigations have proven that the physical senses can be reproduced by the mind alone. Do we not know of a mental communication between friends which is independent of the ear? Is this not soul communication? Cannot the mind again retravel the steps that the feet have taken? And so it is with all the senses; God's world is not limited to one plane.

THE RESURRECTION BODY

"In my Father's house are many mansions." But will our mansion in the future life be a definite one? Will our bodies be real and solid as they now are? We cannot imagine a body without clear outline and contour of form. Shall we simply be spirits, void of definiteness of shape? We *are* spirits right now, just as much as we ever shall, or ever can be. Spirits using a definite body through which to express the life we feel and know. We are spirits now and we shall be spirits then. As life has given us a body through which to function here so will it give us a body through which to function hereafter.

Have we not already been told of a matter, or a fine substance more subtle than that which appears? Has not science told us that within *all* matter, as we understand it, there is a finer, more subtle, yet more solid substance than the matter we are ordinarily aware of? This inner matter has just as much possibility of taking on form as the outer matter, indeed, we are told that all form comes from it. The resurrection body will be taken with us when we leave this one behind.

SELF-RECOGNITION
IS ETERNAL

But shall we remember *ourselves* when the veil has been torn apart and we have deserted this form of clay? Do we remember from one day to another while here? Certainly, that silent thread of memory, linking one event to another in perfect and logical sequence is not a physical, but a mental thing and will be carried with us. The dead die not, but live in complete recognition of themselves.

We shall remain, as we now are, self-conscious beings. We remember yesterday, we are conscious of today and anticipate tomorrow. All that is mental and spiritual, alive and aware, goes with us beyond the grave. "O death, where is thy sting? O grave, where is thy victory?"

But will our friends know us when they too are gathered on that fairer shore of eternal life? Do they not recognize us now? Is it the body which recognizes the body or the mind which recognizes the body? Lifeless bodies do not salute one another. It is the seer who sees, the knower who knows. All else is effect.

THE OUTWARD-BOUND SOUL

Death is a gateway of the onward and outbound soul, into higher expressions of life, truth and beauty. The eternal mandate of Spirit is progression; it must be expressed in greater and still greater modes of livingness. The spirit of man must move on from heights to greater heights of self-expression and self-realization; ever moving nearer to the Heart of All.

Paul knew and understood these things and was trying to teach his followers that they need not fear death. Every great religious and philosophic teaching, given to the world, has accepted the necessity of the immortality of the soul and the eternity of the Spirit of every man. Only the uninstructed have feared the hereafter.

. .
.

Where the Spirit of the Lord is, there is liberty.

But we all, with open face beholding as in a glass the glory of the Lord,

Are changed into the same image from glory to glory, even as by the Spirit of the Lord.

II CORINTHIANS 3

. .
.

THE LAW OF GOD IS ONE OF LIBERTY

The law of God is one of liberty and not one of bondage. The Spirit of the Lord is everywhere. Freedom and liberty are also everywhere if we could but see them. Freedom, like the Truth, is self-existent and self-propelling. The Spirit, Truth and Freedom are coexistent with one another.

Whenever we are conscious of God or pure Spirit we are made free. This is proven in mental and spiritual healing; when we are conscious of perfect life the body is healed. We must become unconscious of the imperfect and conscious of the perfect alone. Since our ideas of perfection are limited to our present understanding we do not yet manifest perfection. With a greater unfoldment of reality through our consciousness we shall evolve a more perfect body.

In the demonstration of abundance, we seek to realize the liberty of the Sons of God; the freedom whereby God proves His absoluteness. This is done, not by meditation upon limitation, but by contemplating plenty, abundance, success, prosperity, and happiness.

It is unscientific to dwell upon lack for it will create the undesired condition. It *is* scientific to meditate on plenty, to bring the mind to a point of conceiving an eternal flow of life, truth, and energy through us and through everything that we do, say or think.

HOW TO DEMONSTRATE LIBERTY

To demonstrate liberty, drop all negative thoughts from the mind. Do not dwell upon adversity but think plenty into everything, for there is power in the word. Meditate on the things you are doing as being already done—complete and perfect.

Try to sense the Infinite Life around and within you. This Life is already fully expressed and complete. This Life is your life now and the life of all that you do, say, or think. Meditate upon this life until your whole being flows into It and becomes one with It.

Now you are ready to prove your principle by allowing this Life to flow through the thing that you are working on or for. Do not will or try to compel things to happen. Things happen by immutable law and you do not need to energize the essence of being; it is already big with power; all you need to do is realize this fact, then let it be done unto you or unto that which you are working for. Let, is a big word and an important one. By taking thought you do not add one cubit to Reality, but you do allow Reality to manifest in the things you are doing.

As the power of your meditation is centered on what you are doing, life flows through that thing, animating it with real power and action which culminates in the desired result. The Spirit of God is loosed in your work; where this Spirit is, there is liberty.

"But we all, with open face beholding as in a glass the glory of the Lord, are changed into the same image from glory to glory, even as by the Spirit of the Lord."

MENTAL EXPANSION

As our thought is opened and we behold the image of eternity within ourselves, we are changed by this image into a newness of life. This is accomplished by the Spirit of God.

The subjective state of thought is the creative medium within us, which fact psychology has proven beyond any question of doubt. Emerson tells us that we are inlets and might become outlets to the Divine Nature. We already are inlets, but we must consciously become outlets. A great mystic tells us that the upper part of the soul is merged with God and the lower part with time and conditions. Plotinus tells us that when the soul looks to God alone for its inspiration, its work is done better even though its back is turned to its work. And Jesus tells us to seek the Kingdom of God first and that all else will be added unto us.

Now the image of God is imprinted upon each one of us and all reflect the Divine Glory to some degree. Indeed we are part of the Divine Glory. When our thought is turned from limitation to the greater glory we reflect that glory.

When the subjective state of our thought receives its images from reality, it, in turn, reflects this reality into all that we do. Gradually, as this process takes place, the outer man becomes changed and as his concepts become enlarged, so his conditions and physique take on a newness of life.

And this change in the outer is brought about by the Spirit of God. The Spirit of God, being the One and only Presence in the universe, brings about events and remolds conditions after its own likeness.

THE ASCENDING SCALE OF LIFE

We are changed from glory to glory. This implies that the divine scale is ever ascending. There is no end to the Divine Nature and therefore no end to the possibility of our expressing It. But we must behold It, we must look steadfastly into this reality if we are to image it in our own minds.

Here is no forlorn outlook, no limited concept! All that God has or Is, belongs to us and is ours to make use of; we are not to separate Life from living but unite the two into a perfect One; the Thing and the way it works; the glory, and the image of the glory in common affairs of everyday life. Nor hath eye seen nor can tongue tell the greater possibility of any soul. Only God has revealed this through His Son. And this Son is each one of us, from the apparent least to the apparent greatest.

The world is saturated with divinity, immersed in reality, and filled with possibility. We must take this divine possibility and mold it into a present actuality in everyday experience. This is the way to freedom, the pathway to peace and happiness.

. .
.

We are troubled on every side, yet not distressed;
We are perplexed, but not in despair;
Persecuted, but not forsaken; cast down, but not destroyed;
For which cause we faint not; but though our outward man
    perish, yet the inward man is renewed day by day.
For our light affliction, which is but for a moment, worketh
    for us a far more exceeding and eternal weight of glory;
While we look not at the things which are seen, but at things
    which are not seen:
For the things which are seen are temporal; but the things
    which are not seen are eternal.

II CORINTHIANS 4

. .
.

THE DIVINE IDEAS

Even in our troubles we are not cast down and though we appear to be deserted we are not destroyed. All our experiences are working to the end that we learn the lesson of life and return to the Father's House as freed souls.

We should not despise apparent failures, the temporary chagrins of life, for they are salutary, leading the soul to the inner Christ, the Way, the Truth, and the Life. When the experience is complete the lesson will be learned and we shall enter the paradise of contentment.

We do not look at the things which are seen as being eternal. Behind the visible and changeable is the changeless reality, the

Eternal One, working in time and space for the expression of It-self. The Divine Ideas stand back of all human thought, seeking admittance through the doorway of the mind.

If we look at love long enough we shall become lovely, for this is the way of love. God is Love. If we gaze longingly at joy it will make its home with us and we shall enter its portals and be happy. If we seek the divine in men we shall find it and be entertaining angels unawares.

God's ideas and attributes are eternal and cannot change. In change is the changeless. In time is the eternal and timeless. In things the Creator manifests His power and glory forevermore.

∴

For we know that if our earthly house of this tabernacle were
    dissolved,
We have a building of God, an house not made with hands,
    eternal in the heavens.
For in this we groan, earnestly desiring to be clothed upon
    with our house which is from heaven:
For we that are in this tabernacle do groan, being burdened:
Not for that we would be unclothed, but clothed upon, that
    mortality might be swallowed up of life.
Wherefore henceforth know we no man after the flesh: yea,
Though we have known Christ after the flesh, yet now
    henceforth know we him no more.

II CORINTHIANS 5

∴

IMMORTAL CLOTHING

This body in which we seem to live is not the eternal body. We have a body not made with hands, eternal in the heavens. As our thought reaches up and on to that greater truth we are clothed upon from heaven. That is, we more perfectly pattern the Divine and consequently more completely manifest the eternal.

We do not wish to be "unclothed, but clothed upon." This is an interesting concept, for it implies that immortality clothes itself in definite forms, more beautiful than those which now appear.

We are to know no man after the flesh but even Christ after the Spirit. Thus are we swallowed up of life. Death is overcome not by dwelling upon it, but by contemplating eternal life. It is the belief of the writer that should one become completely unconscious of death and all fear of it, one would never know that he died even though he went through the experience of passing from this life to the next. Death would be swallowed up of life.

It seems probable that when the last enemy is overcome we shall pass from one experience to another at will, that the soul will clothe itself in a body on whatever plane it finds itself, a body which will express the soul on that plane. We are to know no man after the flesh but after the Spirit.

· ·
·

I bow my knee unto the Father of our Lord Jesus Christ,
Of whom the whole family in heaven and earth is named,
That he would grant you, according to the riches of his glory,
To be strengthened with might by his Spirit in the inner man;
That Christ may dwell in your hearts by faith; that ye, being
    rooted and grounded in love,

May be able to comprehend with all saints what is the
breadth, and length, and depth, and height;
And to know the love of Christ, which passeth knowledge,
That ye might be filled with all the fullness of God.
Now unto him that is able to do exceeding abundantly above
all that we ask or think, according to that power that
worketh in us,
Unto him be glory in the church by Christ Jesus throughout
all ages, world without end.

EPHESIANS 3

. .
.

THE INNER MAN

"To be strengthened with might by his Spirit in the inner man." The
inner man is Christ and Christ is the son of God. This inner man is
revealed by what he does. As we do not see God, so we do not see
the real man. We never see causes, only effects, but the effect guar-
antees the nature of its cause.

The Spirit of God dwells in the inner man with power and
might. The outer man reflects this Spirit in so far as the intellect al-
lows it to come forth into expression.

When Christ dwells in us in love—which is unity, we are able
to understand the things that the saints have understood. *Saint* simply means an unusually wise and good man—all the saints have
been human beings just as we are, for God makes all people alike.
The universe plays no favorites.

To be filled with the fullness of God is to manifest our true nature, which is Christ, the son of God—"the power that worketh in

us." This power is the power of God, and if we admitted no other we should ever be satisfied, happy, prosperous, well, and complete.

THE ENDLESS CREATION

"World without end." This refers to the endless creation of the Almighty. Particular worlds will always begin and end, as do cabbages and kings, but creation itself, the necessity of God's manifesting Himself in time and space, will never end. If creation could end, then God would end: as this is unthinkable, it follows that "world without end," or worlds without end, are necessary to the expression of the Spirit.

. .
.

I therefore, the prisoner of the Lord, beseech you that ye
walk worthy of the vocation wherewith ye are called,
With all lowliness and meekness, with long-suffering, for-
bearing one another in love;
Endeavoring to keep the unity of the Spirit in the bond of
peace.
There is one body, and one Spirit, even as ye are called in one
hope of your calling;
One Lord, one faith, one baptism, One God and Father of
all, who is above all, and through all, and in you all.
Be renewed in the spirit of your mind; and put on the new
man,
Which after God is created in righteousness and true holiness.
Let all bitterness, and wrath, and anger, and clamor, and evil
speaking, be put away from you, with all malice:

And be ye kind one to another, tender-hearted, forgiving one another.

EPHESIANS 4

• •
•

THE UNITY OF LIFE

The unity of the Spirit is kept through the bonds of peace. Other than peace suggests confusion and separation. The Spirit is a perfect unit and we harmonize with this unity when we maintain a state of peace in our minds.

"There is one body and one Spirit." The entire creation is this body, the body of God who is One Spirit. Within this one body are all bodies; that is, within the one creation—which is the product of the one Spirit—are all bodies.

We have learned that all material forms come from one ultimate substance. Any special body is some manifestation of this original stuff. The original substance takes many forms; multiplicity, or many within unity, or the One.

"One Lord, one faith, one baptism." One Lord, who is the indwelling Christ, generic man or the universal Son. There is but one faith, for faith is an affirmative mental attitude toward the universe, and one baptism which is the realization that we are in One Spirit.

"One God and Father of all, who is above all, and through all, and in you all." It would be impossible to make a clearer statement of truth: One life *behind* all that lives—one, one, one, and never two. The unity of all life. To learn this is to know the secret of the ages. The wisest man who ever lived knew no more than this about reality, and we are as wise as the wisest when *we know it.*

Here is a mystical saying: God is in all, through all and above all, which means we partake of the One Life but we are not *all* of this Life. No man can exhaust the Divine Nature but all live by, in, and through It. It is in us but also above us. We shall ever ascend into a greater expression of this One but we can never completely encompass It. This is a glorious concept, and one which fills us with wonder at the majesty of our own being—forever hid with Christ in God.

THE RENEWING OF THE MIND

We are told to be renewed in mind by the Spirit and to put on the new man which is created in true holiness. Religious Science teaches how to accomplish this. The mind is the creative factor within us and when the mind takes its pattern after the Spirit it automatically renews the outer man after true holiness or wholeness.

Whatever the mind holds to and firmly believes in, forms a new pattern of thought within its creative mold; as whatever thought is held in the mind tends to take outward form in new creations. This is the secret, and the whole secret of the creative law of mind.

· ·
·

Finally, my brethren, be strong in the Lord, and in the power
of his might.
Put on the whole armor of God, that ye may be able to stand
against the wiles of the devil.
For we wrestle not against flesh and blood, but against principalities, against powers, against the rulers of the dark-

ness of this world, against spiritual wickedness in high places.

Wherefore take unto you the whole armor of God, that ye may be able to withstand in the evil day, and having done all, to stand.

Stand therefore, having your loins girt with truth, and having on the breastplate of righteousness;

And your feet shod with the preparation of the gospel of peace;

Above all, taking the shield of faith, wherewith ye shall be able to quench all the fiery darts of the wicked.

And take the helmet of salvation, and the sword of the Spirit, which is the word of God.

EPHESIANS 6

"BE STRONG IN THE LORD"

"Be strong in the Lord, and in the power of his might." To be strong in the Lord is to be sure of ourselves because we are *sure of the Principle of life which manifests Itself through us.*

We wrestle not against outward things but against inward ideas and beliefs. The power of darkness is the power of false belief and superstition. If a man can change his inner concept his whole life will be changed. All cause is from within, all effect is forever without.

WICKEDNESS IN HIGH PLACES

Wickedness in high places means an inverted use of the law of righteousness, the misuse of the powers of the mind. The mental law is neutral, plastic, receptive, and creative. There is a right and a wrong use of this law, just as there is a right and wrong use of any other law.

THE ARMOR OF GOD

The armor of God is faith in the good, the enduring, and the true. Against such there is no law. That is, against truth nothing can stand. The armor of God suggests protection to those who believe in and trust the law of Good. With this armor—knit together by that thread of unity running through all, strong with the strength of the Almighty, burnished with clear vision and true estimates of life and reality—we are safe. We abide under the shadow of the everlasting Truth. With Moses we can say, "underneath are the everlasting arms."

The breastplate of righteousness covers and gives sanctuary to the heart of hearts, the innermost soul of man. The feet, shod with the gospel of peace, can travel and not become weary; for "His ways are pleasant ways and all His paths are paths of peace."

And the shield of faith shall quench the fiery darts of the wicked. The positive thought of truth is a shield against which nothing, unlike itself, can stand. In Religious Science we learn that no thought of negation can enter a mind already filled with peace and faith. The suggestion of limitation, fear and doubt cannot find entrance to that mental home where God is enthroned as the supreme guest.

And the sword of God is the word of Truth. This has also been called the two-edged sword, cleaving the false from the true, cutting its way across the path of confusion, uprooting the thistles and briars, clearing the way for truth and beauty to flourish in the home of the soul.

The word of Spirit is not a battle hymn of righteousness, but a paean of praise, a psalm of beauty and a song of joy. "If God be with us, who can be against us?"

. .

Let this mind be in you, which was also in Christ Jesus; who, being in the form of God, thought it not robbery to be equal with God;

For it is God which worketh in you both to will and to do of his good pleasure.

PHILIPPIANS 2

. .

THE MIND THAT JESUS USED

We are to let the mind be in us which was in Christ Jesus. Note the way the expression is used. The mind which was in Christ Jesus. This means the Mind of God. Not our personal mind—marvelous as this is with all its different ramifications—but the mind which Jesus used; the Divine Mind of the creator and ruler of the universe.

To have the same mind that Jesus used implies a power which is available to all and may be used by all. The mind which was in

Christ Jesus was the Truth; hence, he became the way. But we also are to become the way and this can be accomplished only when we use the same mind that he used, which is the Mind of God.

We have the mind of Christ in such degree as we trust implicitly in the universe and no longer do those things which contradict the fundamental goodness. From this mind proceeds the perfect law, which is a law of liberty.

This mind is God working in and through us. God can work for us only by working through us. Consequently there is no other name under heaven whereby man may become saved—not the *name* of Jesus but the *Mind of Christ*. The individual is thrown back upon himself and upon the universe. Every man has the mind of Christ if he will admit it, but he can use this mind only when he is in harmony with life. Nature always guards herself against any undue approaches and the righteous alone may enter the portals of Truth.

. .

Finally, brethren, whatsoever things are true, whatsoever things are honest, whatsoever things are just, whatsoever things are pure, whatsoever things are lovely, whatsoever things are of good report; if there be any virtue, and if there be any praise, think on these things.
I can do all things through Christ which strengtheneth me.
God shall supply all your needs according to his riches in glory by Christ Jesus.

PHILIPPIANS 4

. .

A PATTERN FOR THOUGHT

We are to think on those things which are of good report. That is, we are to think on those things which are of the Truth. When we do this, we can accomplish because of our own inner mind which is Christ. This mind is the creator of the heavens and the earth and all that dwell therein.

And God will supply all our needs. This is a beautiful thought, to be fed from the table of the universe whose board is ever spread with blessedness and peace, whose loving-kindness has never been fathomed, whose grace and truth are the cornerstones of reality. We are to be fed, clothed, and supplied in every need straight from the center and source of all.

More than this we could not ask. Greater could not be given. Lowell tells us that "Heaven alone is given away," and all is ours for the asking. Shall not this asking, then, include all righteousness and truth?

* *
*

See that none render evil for evil unto any man, but ever follow that which is good, both among yourselves, and to all
   men.
Rejoice evermore. Pray without ceasing. In every thing give
   thanks:
Quench not the Spirit. Despise not prophesyings. Prove all
   things: hold fast that which is good.
Abstain from all appearance of evil. And the very God of
   peace sanctify you wholly.

I Thessalonians 5

* *
*

REJOICE EVERMORE

We are to rejoice evermore. There is no sadness in the Spirit, It is ever happy and free, for It knows neither depression nor confusion and we belong to It, are in and of It. We are to rejoice evermore.

CONSTANT PRAYER

"Pray without ceasing." This means to be always on the affirmative side of life. To pray without ceasing is to doubt never, but to always trust in the law of good. This inner communion is essential to the soul and natural to the mind. It is a constant recognition of our relationship to that Presence in which we live, move and have our being.

"In every thing give thanks." An attitude of gratitude is most salutary and bespeaks the realization that we are *now* in heaven. How we love to do for those who cooperate with and are grateful for our small endeavors. Gratitude is one of the chief graces of human existence and is crowned in heaven with a consciousness of unity.

"QUENCH NOT THE SPIRIT"

"Quench not the Spirit." We are not to be ashamed of our trust in God nor are we to deny the inner light that lights every man's reason to the ultimate reason of all. Spiritual emotion is common to all people and is one of the ways through which the Spirit works. When this emotion is blocked it hinders the currents of life from flowing and the result is stagnation. In psychology we learn that congested emotions are disastrous to health. If this is true of the physical emotions how much more must it be true of those higher emotions which are altogether spiritual. What is true on one plane is true on all. There are ascending scales of being and each reproduces the one next above or next below. But, from the highest to the lowest, each plane partakes of the nature of the whole, since all are in, and of, it. If physical emotions, unexpressed, can congest the subjective thought—producing mental and *physical* confusion, and they can—it follows that unexpressed *spiritual* emotions can congest the soul and hinder a more complete flow of life through the individual. This in accordance with law.

If the artist suppressed all spiritual emotion he would never be a great artist. In art we call this emotion—temperament—in oratory we call it inspiration, and in purely spiritual things we call it illumination. Somewhere the soul must stand naked to the Truth if it is to receive it in all its fullness. There must be an outlet as well as an inlet if there is to be a continual flow. "Quench not the Spirit," but let the intellect decide what the emotions are to respond to. This is the secret of a well-balanced life.

"Prove all things: hold fast that which is good." We are not to be afraid of strange ideas or doctrines, but are to prove them and accept only that which is true. We are to analyze, dissect, and investigate until we know the truth and then we are to hold fast to it. In this way all advance must come, whether in science, philosophy, religion, or in anything else.

If any of you lack wisdom, let him ask of God, that giveth to all men liberally, and upbraideth not; and it shall be given him.

But let him ask in faith, nothing wavering. For he that wavereth is like a wave of the sea driven with the wind and tossed.

For let not that man think that he shall receive any thing of the Lord.

A double-minded man is unstable in all his ways.

Let no man say when he is tempted, I am tempted of God: for God cannot be tempted with evil, neither tempteth he any man;

But every man is tempted, when he is drawn away of his own lust, and enticed. Do not err, my beloved brethren.

Every good gift and every perfect gift is from above, and cometh down from the Father of lights, with whom is no variableness, neither shadow of turning.

But be ye doers of the word, and not hearers only, deceiving your own selves.

Pure religion and undefiled before God and the Father is this,

To visit the fatherless and widows in their affliction and to keep himself unspotted from the world.

JAMES 1

* *
*

ASK IN FAITH, BELIEVING

If we lack wisdom we are to come to the source of all knowledge and we shall receive it. But how are we to ask? In faith, believing. A double-minded man gets nowhere. How true this is! God can give us only what we take, and since the taking is a mental act, we can take only what we believe we already have. This is in accord with the teaching of Jesus, that when we pray we must believe we already have the answer to our prayer.

God gives to us by being the thing, in us, that we ask for. If we deny this inner being, the Spirit cannot make the gift. Anything that is not of faith is sin or a mistake, as we are told in another passage of this book of wisdom.

Faith in God and in ourselves should be consciously generated. All trouble comes from disbelief in the universe, followed by wrong acts which are the result of disbelief and ignorance of the law of good, which is a law of liberty.

The lesson is simple enough. When we ask for anything, we are to believe that we have it, but we are to ask for that which is in unity with life. This unity includes, health, happiness, and success. These are native to the atmosphere of God and to the atmosphere of the inner man, which is Christ. Let us dislodge doubt, fear, and unbelief and trust implicitly in Good.

EVIL IS CREATED BY MAN

Very emphatically the writer tells us that God never tempts any man. He says that God cannot be tempted and that all temptation is from our own minds. It could not be stated any plainer. Evil is *man created,* while God, the Eternal Goodness, knows nothing about it. He is too pure to behold evil and cannot look upon it. Evil is the direct and suppositional opposite to good and has no reality behind it or actual law to come to its support. God tempts no man. It is a mistake to say that God tries us to see if we are fit to enter the kingdom of heaven. God never tries any one.

We make our own mistakes and suffer from our own foolishness, and we must also make our own return journey into righteousness. God was, is and will remain, the essence of life, truth, and purity. Let us enter this essence in belief and be freed from our unbelief and human mistakes.

All goodness and every good gift comes from the Father of light. Darkness has no father, but is an illegitimate child of superstition and unbelief, having no parentage in Reality. The universe is not divided against itself. The good teacher said, "A house divided against itself cannot stand."

There is no shadow of turning in the Truth. It is just what It is and there can be nothing either added to or taken from It. It is One and never two. We enter the One through a conscious unity with It.

DOERS OF THE WORD

"But be ye doers of the word, and not hearers only, deceiving your own selves." This should teach us not to make idle talk about our understanding. What we *know* we can *do.* What we cannot do we only suppose. Unused knowledge is suppositional and unreal; it is an assumption and as such never produced anything. Not everyone who says Lord, Lord, but those who *do* the will of Truth, enter in.

We but deceive ourselves when we boast about our understanding and are not able to prove that we possess any. A silent conviction is worth more than the loudest proclamation from the housetops, of those who shout affirmations to the great nowhere. An ounce of conviction is worth many pounds of affirmation.

Pure religion manifests itself through acts of kindness and mercy. It is not arrogant—claiming a front seat in heaven—but humble before the great Whole. It unifies with all humanity and finds no great difference between saint and sinner. Such a religion as this the sad old world needs, for it is sick of pretense and would like a practical demonstration of a belief in God made manifest through good works.

．．
．

If ye fulfill the royal law according to the scripture, Thou
    shalt love thy neighbor as thyself, ye do well:
But if ye have respect to persons, ye commit sin, and are con-
    vinced of the law as transgressors.

JAMES 2

．．
．

THE LAW IS NO RESPECTER OF PERSONS

James speaks about being convinced of the law as transgressors. He does not say that God is convinced we are transgressors, but that the law is convinced. This passage is filled with meaning. God is natural Goodness, eternal Freedom, and pure loving-kindness. But the law is a cold, hard fact, returning to each the result of his own acts, be they false or true. The law is a neutral but an intelligent force, a doer, and not a knower. All law is of the same nature.

When we do wrong the law punishes. When we do right it rewards. Everything is according to law and order; this is the only way the universe could function. If our thought is of God, or Good, we shall be using the law in the right way. When our thought and act are opposed to God, or Good, we transgress and are punished. "There is no sin but a mistake and no punishment but a consequence." In like manner Emerson tells us "there is no sin but ignorance," and this is true, for, if we knew the Truth, we should not misuse the law.

The law is no respecter of persons and will bring good or evil to any, according to his use or misuse of it. It will be a law of freedom to the righteous and one of bondage to those who misuse it. We cannot escape from the creative power of our thought and there is no use in trying to do so. All we need do is to use the law from the right motive, then we shall be made free.

. .
.

And the prayer of faith shall save the sick, and the Lord shall
  raise him up;
And if he have committed sins, they shall be forgiven him.
Confess your faults one to another, and pray one for another,
  that ye may be healed.
The effectual fervent prayer of a righteous man availeth much.

JAMES 5

. .
.

THE PRAYER OF FAITH

The prayer of faith is an unconditioned belief in both the ability and the desire of Spirit to hear and answer. The prayer of faith heals the sick through the law which says that whatever images of thought are held in the subjective side of mind will tend to appear in the body.

When the prayer of faith penetrates the subjective thought and neutralizes false images then the sick are raised into health. Even God cannot heal the sick unless this psychological change takes place in the inner creative thought. All is love but all is law: one balances the other. Law cannot and will not depart from its nature.

When we pray, believing, we erase false ideas from our inner thought, then the Spirit can make the gift of health. When we admit the light, it comes in, since there is no way it could enter except through a receptive mind.

If we could give up our diseases—offer them on the altar of faith, to the giver of all life—we would be healed. It is not easy to release our troubles; we are prone to linger with them. But, by effectual and fervent prayer, we gradually loose false thought into its native nothingness. God is perfect life and when we enter His light we are healed.

THE CONFESSION OF MISTAKES

James tells us to confess our faults. This thought suggests one of the great psychological truths of the inner nature. Psychoanalysis—which is the analysis of the soul or subjective mind—is a scientific method for the erasure of false beliefs. It is often forgiveness of sins done in a scientific manner.

Our minds are burdened with many things. Often our religions, which should automatically balance our mentalities, suppress them, and create morbidness on the subjective side of thought. This happens when we feel condemned for our mistakes. The Bible tells us that God will blot out these mistakes and remember them no more against us forever. This is complete removal and erasure of all mistakes. How could it be different? God is of pure eye and perfect mind; He is perfect Spirit. When we enter this Spirit and bare our souls to Its great light we loose our troubles and are healed.

The confession of sins, or mistakes, helps us to let go of troubles and to feel that the universe holds nothing against us. Sin means making a mistake, and while we continue to make them we continue to perpetuate their dire results. We should come daily to the Spirit of Goodness for a complete washing away of all mistakes, fears, and troubles.

The man who feels that his mistakes can be blotted out is in a better psychological position than the one who thinks God will not forgive. We should learn to let go of our mistakes and remember them no longer against ourselves. Nothing is gained by holding to past errors. The best thing to do is to let go of and forget them altogether.

It is scientific to consciously let go all our troubles, it is most unwise to hold on to them. Some will say it is right that we should suffer for our past errors. It is right that we should suffer; we already have done so and will continue to do so until we pay the last farthing. But the last farthing is paid when we let go and trust in the law of Good.

It is impossible for a sane person to believe that God delights in condemning or damning anyone. God is natural goodness and eternal Loving-kindness and holds nothing against anyone.

We suffer so long as we make mistakes. We are healed when we come to the Spirit for that cleansing which takes away the mistakes of the world, converting them into great lessons, ever pointing the way to Truth and beauty, to life, health, happiness, and success.

It is scientific for one to consciously let go of his troubles and errors, feeling that they no longer affect him. He has learned the lesson that false ideas do not pay and is willing and glad to turn from all that hurts to the Great Light. And the Spirit, because of its nature of Wholeness, is ever ready to take him in its embrace and make him whole again.

⋅ ⋅
⋅

Behold what manner of love the Father hath bestowed upon
us, that we should be called the sons of God!
Therefore the world knoweth us not, because it knew him not.
Beloved, now are we the sons of God; and it doth not yet appear what we shall be:
But we know that, when he shall appear, we shall be like him;
for we shall see him as he is.
And every man that hath this hope in him purifieth himself,
even as he is pure.
Little children, let no man deceive you: he that doeth righteousness is righteous, even as he is righteous.
For this is the message that ye heard from the beginning, that
we should love one another.
My little children, let us not love in word, neither in tongue;
but in deed, and in truth.

And hereby we know that we are of the truth, and shall as-
sure our hearts before him.

For if our heart condemn us, God is greater than our heart,
and knoweth all things.

And whatsoever we ask, we receive of him, because we keep
his commandments,

And do those things that are pleasing in his sight.

I John 3

∴

"NOW ARE WE
THE SONS OF GOD"

The world does not know the son of God. The material sense cannot recognize the spiritual. Spiritual things must be spiritually understood. God's love is complete in us, in that we are His
sons—the sons of freedom and not of bondage.

"Now are we the sons of God." Not in the hereafter, but in the
Now, are we just what we are, and what we must be—because of
our true natures. "Now are we the Sons of God." The birth of the
soul into the light of Spirit is an awakening to the realization that
God has been with us all the time. "Now are we the sons of God."
Today is the day of complete salvation. Not tomorrow or the day
after, but NOW.

It does not now completely appear what we really are, for now
we see only in part, but when He shall appear we shall recognize
him for we shall see him in his true light. This He, means ourselves—the *Christ in us,* our hope and assurance of eternal glory.

We shall be like him. We have inwardly been like him all the time, but when He shall appear we shall see him as he is, that is, we shall know, even as we also are known; we shall know ourselves.

"We shall see him as he is." Not as he now appears, for he is hidden in the innermost recesses of our nature. We shall see him with the spiritual eye that dims not, with a clear sight that penetrates all suppositional opposites and announces the ever-present reality. We shall see ourselves as we really are, forever held in the bosom of the universe—the sons of God.

Who doeth right, is right, even as *He* is right. This again reveals us to ourselves. This is the great revelation; the revelation of the self to the self. But before this can take place we must have consciously come into our birthright. We must have returned to the Father's House. This return is a conscious act on our part.

When we do right we are right, and when we are right we are like him, for then we shall see Him. This refers to the Christ, indwelling every soul. The son of God in all his beauty and strength.

Even if our own hearts condemn us, we know that the Spirit, which gave the heart, is greater than its gift. God is greater than all human mistakes and in God alone is there peace and happiness. God is natural Goodness and eternal Loving-kindness.

"Who is born of love is born of God, for God is Love." Without love nothing can be accomplished. With love all things are possible. And when we love, our prayers are answered and the gift of heaven is made. The gift of heaven is Life and not death, love and not hate, peace and not confusion.

And we enter this paradise through the gateway of love toward one another and toward God. Love is greater than all else and covers a multitude of mistakes. Love overcomes everything and neutralizes all that is unlike itself. Love is God.

Index

ABOUT THE AUTHOR

Ernest Shurtleff Holmes (1887–1960) was an avid student of the world's spiritual systems. He found in these a common denominator he called the Science of Mind, a practical philosophy for abundant living. Beginning as a self-educated lecturer, Ernest developed a large following of students and went on to formalize his work by founding *Science of Mind* magazine, an educational institute, and the United Church of Religious Science. His writings have inspired the work of countless clergy, business leaders, physicians, and psychologists, and have helped to shape the guiding principles of the modern human potential movement, both spiritual and secular. Born and raised in Maine, Ernest spent much of his adult life in California.